WHAT PEOPLE ARE SAYING ABOUT

BEYOND THE FURTHEST EDGE OF NIGHT

Forget dark night of the soul, this book is an account of a dark *life* of the soul. Cliff Gogh's book opens on a mind beset by terror. The mystic's journey is through the valley ⸱⸱ ⸱he shadows of death but opens, inevitably, into lu⸱⸱⸱ ⸱nscendence. Terror yields to the sublime. Th⸱ ⸱olden light that penetrates the darkest ⸱⸱ ⸱s and the collective unconsciou⸱ ⸱apped by fear, Gogh concludes. ⸱ ⸱ force that peers from beyond the veil w⸱ ⸱e. Come! The journey begins.
Catlyn Keenan Ph.D., author of *Strip*

A wounded man, alone, adrift, alienated: by night he walks deserted streets and forest trails, painfully conscious of his inability to fit into society, unable even to speak to another human being. You might expect his course to be a downward spiral. But unexpectedly, by embracing his personal darkness, by journeying clear-eyed to the furthest edge of night, author Cliff Gogh finds his way to a profound and transforming acceptance of life just as it is.
Tim Ward, author of *Indestructible You: Building a Self That Can't Be Broken* and *What the Buddha Never Taught*

Beyond the Furthest Edge of Night is astonishingly unique. It grabbed me like the jaws of a rabid wolverine; had I wanted to, I'm not sure I could have escaped once I had read the first pages. Mr. Gogh's experience as a disconnected youth is disturbing, but authenticity drips from the page. This unique story plays with time, and the narrator wanders from the inner psyche to the outer trails of city and forest as if tramping freely on the rails.

Like all mystics, even deeply wounded ones like Mr. Gogh, he discovers eternal truths, such as when examining a tiny leaf that reveals the sublime wonder of everything in the cosmos, from matter to mind to spirit. Many of the images described in the book affected my mind like either a deadly virus or a saving light in the darkness of existential despair. The truth of this work is that to be free, actually free, we must confront and look into the eyes of our pain. If we look hard without flinching, we can catch a glimpse of the totality of love before it slips away to be lost again. Mr. Gogh's realizations teeter precariously on the edge until the moment comes when separation ceases and the body fades away into the ocean of eternity.

Neil Richardson, founder of the online virtual commons Walt Whitman Integral, author of *Episodic Flash Sight* and 'Walt Whitman's Vision for a New Person and a New Democracy', Director of Advancement, Partnerships and Continuing Education at the University of the District of Columbia Community College

Like Dante's *Divine Comedy* and its description of the Inferno, *Beyond the Furthest Edge of Night* is a modern autobiography by a spiritual vagabond. It is a journey that alternates between the dark and the radiant, one that goes from nihilistic, suicidal despair to Mr. Gogh's enduring reverence for all of life. This is a poetic interior journey that is not for the faint of heart. Gogh's descriptions of the agony of his dark night of the soul before his shadow self is brought into the light are surrealistically vivid. His profound catharsis leads to a recognition of the timeless unconditioned spirit in all of existence. This is an account by a self-avowed renunciate who is in the world but not of it.

Ira Rechtshaffer Ph.D., author of *Mindfulness and Madness*

Beyond the Furthest Edge of Night

Beyond the Furthest Edge of Night

Cliff Gogh

**CHANGE
MAKERS
BOOKS**

Winchester, UK
Washington, USA

First published by Changemakers Books, 2016
Changemakers Books is an imprint of John Hunt Publishing Ltd., Laurel House, Station Approach,
Alresford, Hants, SO24 9JH, UK
office1@jhpbooks.net
www.johnhuntpublishing.com
www.changemakers-books.com

For distributor details and how to order please visit the 'Ordering' section on our website.

Text copyright: Cliff Gogh 2015

ISBN: 978 1 78535 295 9
Library of Congress Control Number: 2015950497

A CIP catalogue record for this book is available from the British Library.

Design: Stuart Davies

Printed in the USA by Edwards Brothers Malloy

We operate a distinctive and ethical publishing philosophy in all
areas of our business, from our global network of authors to
production and worldwide distribution.

1

Lethargy defines my life. I wake late in the afternoon, if I don't sleep all day. It came over me in my adolescence, verging on exhaustion, a tiredness too strong to fight. If I explain my life, maybe it'll become clear why I'm so tired. At the end of a decade, I look back to see I've slept through most of it, usually unwilling to get up in the morning.

However, sometimes I'm seized by a feeling. It might last for hours. Peace of mind comes into my senses and intense concentration enlivens them, like I've taken a seaside journey, walked beside the whole depths of the ocean, the currents and the life, the infinite creatures and the submerged quiet, in the midst of a storm, with howling wind and lightning. It produces a strong sense of significance, an opiate of sorts, and this feeling throbs in my limbs and my brain. I'm usually not so supremely happy, but sometimes I feel this uncanny elation and it crazes me like an ecstatic religious experience. It's calm. It's furiously peaceful. A cheerful, patient aura of rapture coming from something universal: If I could put it into words, maybe it would last forever. I seem to understand something hidden, the essential goodness of the universe.

I tend to call it being. It's the deeper self when all the surface difficulties and upsets no longer have power. I feel a presence, like stillness amidst a tornado, the eye of the storm that's forever there waiting. It comes with the mental acuity of a deep, long, thoughtful dream. If I have a purpose, mine is to delve down through the shadows and return to the surface with this being.

The first of such elated experiences occurred when I was still quite young, as I observed the stars. I sat looking out the window of my parents' car. Somewhere outside that window, I felt myself floating in space. I was lulled by the car's engine, and the magical universe reverberated right along with it. A great multitude of stars stretched everywhere overhead, infinite, and the sight made me feel alive. The stars radiated mathematics; they hummed with the magnificent magnitude of existence. A feeling of benevolence came and gathered around me, and I drew close to it, as close to it as I'd ever been. I know now what it was, though at the time I just let it be. It was the unmistakable euphoria that comes when awake to the inner being. It leaves a comfortable lassitude in the limbs and the sense that everything will be all right.

But things returned to normal. It wasn't a lasting happiness. It never is. By the time the night was over, I was back to my childhood self, nervous. My family was out in public, visiting a carnival. We were surrounded by a crowd. People stopped here and there to look at the prizes on display, and they meandered in lines up and down the fairgrounds. In public, I was in the habit of burying myself. When I saw another young boy walking before us with his family, I felt the urge to remove myself from the open air. When we passed other families, parents eating pretzels and children holding stuffed animals, I wanted only to fade into hiding somewhere where I could be alone. That was my regular state. From my earliest years, I felt like a tiny voice in a crowd of the self-assured. According to my own estimation, I was deficient. My anxiety was built upon the feeling of inferiority. I'd been sick with the feeling since the very beginning.

Throughout my adolescence, I was the same. My social experiences left me feeling awkward, and my demeanor conveyed oddness, an inescapable impression I left. In the street, my nervous hands hid themselves away in my pockets, like little mice afraid of being seen. And during conversations, my eyes habitually averted themselves or looked up into the sky, as if disinterested, just anywhere but my companion's face. All day I went around absent-minded, totally withdrawn, in the manner of someone who couldn't figure out how to exist like normal people. It startled me every time someone addressed me, maybe because my eyes were constantly shifted downward on my boots. I couldn't find my place in the world; instead, I left to fantasize in dreams or circle about inside my thoughts.

After all these years, I've not changed much in my unusual bearing, but I did change. I wound up keeping the shy mannerisms and the disordered contact with reality, but I've found my self-confidence in my own way. Eventually, dreams became very important; to relinquish the desire to be in the real world and to retire into a private mental landscape, that provided its own alternate form of self-confidence: to be a talented dreamer.

In order to abandon the uncomfortable world, I began to linger about in abstraction. Because the world suffocated me with inhibition, an unrestrained fantasy life proceeded to remove me from it for release. It was the natural result of my anxiety to seek some tranquil escape, and my dreams became elaborate, wondrous things to explore in moments when trouble would otherwise have eroded my sense of well-being. I became better and better at dreaming, entering the invisible every time I felt uneasy. Over the years, I refined my fantasies, gliding along languidly in my thoughts, until my gestures were either feeble with hypnotism or ethereal with half-sleep.

These days, my methods are those of a ghost. I've haunted the periphery of life for countless years, meditating on my private sanctuary and my uncertain beliefs, which are a lack of beliefs. My beliefs shift, always, then return to the center, to non-belief. All the while, it's been impossible to strain myself in order to exist in social circles. I've tried on occasion and it ends in solitude. Solitude is far easier to deal with for someone who practically speaks in a whisper. And anyway, dreams are a magical world to live in. Sometimes when I sleep I dream unexpected and impossible things. They are such unusual dreams that I often abandon life to recline in bed for thirty hours.

I dreamt once of being taken down a river by a man in a dark robe. He rowed our small boat beneath an archway, silently, and at the moment we passed through the archway, a flight of doves scattered above us into the air. We entered a domed enclosure and arrived shortly at a great work of architecture hidden at the end of the river. It was a university, a magnificent one, like an ancient castle of mossy stone, and a strange one: Dark-robed scholars dwelt within, working on projects inspired by self-searching and seeking for the sublime. They were students of the meaning of life. Their long, hideous fingers were scanning the pages of withered books. Just as we arrived, they all left. They headed off on a journey into the dark, dismal landscape outside the university. They turned at the foot of the mountains and said to me, entreating me to follow: "Come with us, to anything that can ever be known."

I live a strange life, half removed from reality. It's nice to become a phosphorescence, a little ethereal speck barely noticeable in the ordinary world. Ghostliness has its own rewards. I consider what life is, and I delve into my being, like a sleepy diver searching for treasures. Countless nights I've discovered new things. It's that late-night solitude in which the metaphysical and the mystical conjoin. The beyond breathes its sweet breath near to my skin. I feel the same feeling I felt as a child, the peace of mind and the elated awe for the majestic universe. The intangible comes closer and closer until the eye of the tornado is seen as a penetrating soul, an interpenetrating soul, the presence of being, a behemoth of all beings.

2

I remember being very young, lying in my bed, considering my future. It was a desperate future I imagined. I'd seen myself being worn away, like a wound rubbed against with sandpaper, until there was little left of a person. Yet, lying in bed, I made the decision to be gentle. It was in stark contrast to my father to be soft. If the world and life demanded a certain hardness of heart, my reaction was to rebel wholeheartedly.

Nearly every night, my father stood with his face just a few inches from mine and spat insults about my incompetence at me. You aren't fit. You aren't capable of living a life. If I defended myself, the attack would become physical. He would throw me around the room, push me down, slap me, until I quieted, grew passive, and listened to a further hour of belligerent screaming.

One evening, he entered the family room to discover my shoes on the new wooden floor. I had them placed beside me. He'd told me previously not to walk on it in my shoes and I hadn't. The wooden floor was supremely important to him at the time. Under the impression that I had, because my shoes were beside me, he threw me onto the couch, held me down, and proceeded to beat me. I was ten years old, a tiny little thing, and he was quite a lot bigger at thirty-five.

Situations like that occurred day after day, a ritual of lessons that successfully reduced me, like a derogatory schoolteacher with a terrorized student. The message was emphatic: You aren't worth anything compared to me.

The rest is more difficult. I was suicidal. I remember fantasizing about the lightless world after this one: calm, peaceful, without suffering, without hostility or the desperation of victims. At ten, I hung a noose in my garage. Suicide had already become a viable option. I threw a rope over the beams and tied it into a noose. I wanted to see what it would feel like to embrace death. I saw it as a method of escaping the incidents that were shaping my personality, a way to put an end to everything before I had to face the psychological results. I left the noose hanging out there for years. It never moved. Any time I grieved, it served as a reminder.

Life was never satisfactory. An escape was the first thing on my mind. When a young boy knows his future is already broken and will continue to be broken until the end, he'll desire more than all else to put an end to his nightmare. After a bad start, all the decrepit grime of life is too powerful: weakness is the prevailing demeanor; a sickly madness is the outcome, spent in listless paralysis in some hell. I was tired, dispirited: my spirit was broken. Adulthood comes on after a thousand years, far too late. Too much has been ingrained, too much of what leads to bitterness. I'd flailed away against a brick wall too long.

I know enough about suffering to recognize the desperation in the eyes of another and to know with precision from where it arose. Just like in me, I see the tiredness of survivors. The result isn't nice. It goes like this: The wretches punish themselves. The bitter descend into despair again and again. The people walk the streets with sallow faces, their limp hands hanging lifelessly at their sides, having given up hope, having forgotten anything else is possible but their desperate circumstances. That's what I see. I know how it feels. In the eyes of every stranger, I can see a hint of what lies within, down at the core, beneath the hesitation and the self-loathing, where being itself seems to suffer.

For these people, their minds must wonder: Why do I feel so alone, unknown, and bedraggled in the middle of the night?

Some would say that to begin one must annihilate the self and then rebuild the self. Others suggest love is the cure. It's certainly a quest. Life's great quest. To find sympathy for the self, to find love for the whole self, to strive for something that eliminates the pain once and for all. How many countless generations have gone on this quest? It's in religions, art forms, lifestyles. Spiritual experiences are at the heart of it; the sense of being is at the heart of it, lending an outstretched hand to help with the first step. When the feeling comes that life is too hostile, I rededicate myself to the task. To be a dabbler in the spiritual increases peace of mind. To be like a reclusive monk for a month out of the year changes the whole year.

The way for me to begin is to write down myself, to set out on a ruthless, unremitting examination of my own character. Self-examination. I do it once in a while. It's time once again to exit the fake and find what's under the surface, exit the illusory and search for the whole being. I'd like to find the heart of it all by spending some time looking inward. Shame, guilt, fear, feelings of helplessness, the ways in which my mind tricks itself to rise above it all, temporarily, for much needed relief: so many mental states hardly noticed, so many undetected habits, all of them shadows. But deeper lies a magical thing, the deeper being, the unconditioned being. Life's burdens are lessened by a few sessions of self-therapeutic self-examination. For me, self-examination is a self-insurrection, an intellectual suicide, an eye peering into myself in order to untangle the intricate traps of existence in which I've been caught, and a delving downward to the inmost.

I'm engaging in such a self-examination here. The object is to force nothing, to plan nothing, to let thoughts arise of their own accord, as a practitioner of meditation might sit for an hour allowing any thought, without denial of anything, with a fixed eye that doesn't turn away from anything. The thoughts themselves are what dictate my direction. They come from an intuitive understanding, without interference, of what needs to be seen. It's necessary to trust that something deeper inside has a better idea of what I need to see, like an automatic writing exercise in which the unconscious is allowed expression, or a dream that tries to make conscious something as yet unrecognized within. I observe in language my mind working, and the direction plots its own course, with nothing obscured and everything allowed in one prolonged meditation, until I'm carrying on a conversation with myself. I'll continue until I've depleted my energy on every pleasant or unpleasant subject that needs expression, even in the remotest hinterlands of my psyche.

3

My deranged father barked at me to get out of the house, and he meant for good, so I simply left, that very moment, carrying nothing with me, walking out the door at fifteen years old. I vanished into the night. The air was chilly, a windy midwinter night without a single star in the overclouded sky. An old field left the neighborhood in which I'd grown up. It was dry weeds that time of year. I meandered through it for a while, silently, imagining a new life of sleeping in the streets, eating from the dumpsters behind the grocery stores in the city, where there could always be found expired loaves of bread, donuts, and other such perishable foods.

I also felt numb. Since morning, I'd spent the day lying in bed determining whether or not I should kill myself. I'd given up, unhappy with the world as a whole, sick of my insecurity and loneliness and fully prepared to submerge myself in the placid nothingness after life's disappointments. My feelings were deadened from a day spent in despair. All day, I'd essentially held a bottle of pills in my hand, ready to swallow them, and then I'd run into my father. He told me in his loathsome manner that I wasn't welcome in the house anymore.

I went out into the world, unsure if there was a future for me anywhere, feeling the sort of anger a young man feels when rejected at the precise moment he can't stomach any more of life. Memories of my life in that suburban neighborhood went through my thoughts. From the field I could see the houses in a line along the street. Each was invariably lit by a flickering television screen.

I walked aimlessly at first. The weeds thinned more and more as I walked, eventually revealing a train track crossing my path. It went on and on in both directions, toward pinpoints in the distance. I took it, trekked along it without concern for where it led. It was my final exodus out of town, a straight path of immovable steel that left the dismal and connected with the rest of the world.

Soon enough, I found myself in the middle of nowhere. It was a crossroads of sorts. Miles and miles of nothingness expanded from where I stood on the tracks. In every direction was a black distance, a vastness, another world. I watched as the moon appeared from behind the clouds and lit up the dark landscape. The world turned a pale gray in the moonlight, the tracks a mesmerizing silver, luxurious with light, but it was a forgotten world; out there beneath the moon was a world nobody ordinary had ever seen, a world of invalidating loneliness, with old office chairs, garbage bags, and broken television sets dumped here and there like someone's unwanted life.

I wagered that nobody was anywhere for miles. Thus, when I saw a little blue car parked in the dirt, I thought I might sleep inside. When I pulled up at the door handle, however, the man already sleeping inside was alerted. He quickly swatted the car lock, and I hurried away.

I dragged myself along through the night, until morning. The air became extremely cold. I was shivering. When I reached a road, I saw a discarded clump of clothes in the gutter. I examined them and found a worn long-sleeved shirt, light purple, brittle from being left in the rain. I collected it up and dressed myself in it; not so bad, warmer.

When I reached a strip mall, I looked around at the people going to work, to the barbershop, to the pizza restaurant. Life was picking up, carrying on in spite of my situation. The sun was a few inches up on the horizon, but it was still colder than it had been all night.

When I crossed a bridge, I debated jumping off into the electrical wires below. I gazed down into a tangle of them over a shed. They connected with the telephone poles all around. I lingered for a moment at the edge of the bridge, contemplating.

Instead, I went down underneath the bridge. In the dirt, I found a dirtied mattress, and I considered making it my new home. But someone had been living there already. A pornographic magazine lay atop it. Someone's needle. Along the concrete walls beneath the bridge, here and there, was graffiti. Mostly black spray paint: childish satanic symbols, a swastika, and no mention of love.

4

My parents had been in the midst of a divorce. My mother had left my father, tired of his brutishness. Some weeks before, she had begun to arrange for us a new apartment in the next city. I called her at work, and she was horrified that I'd been thrown out. I wound up living with her. My new home would be a little room, all I needed, a bed and a much longed for flight from my previous world. For the rest of the morning, I slept in a field. A great tractor started across it just as I fell asleep. It came upon me and I stood quickly from the dirt. The driver was startled, but I almost saw in his eyes a moment of understanding.

For the next few years, in my new home, I adopted an aloofness from the world. I spent my time up all night wandering outdoors. Soon, I'd succeeded in isolating myself completely, so much so that my character altered significantly. One night, I passed a dead cat that lay in the center of the road, the tires of automobiles running over it one after the other. It was no place to die, so I carried the mangled carcass along the roadway. While I walked along with the thing elevated in my hand, I must have looked frightening. Whatever it was, evidently I was mistaken for someone dangerous. For when I reached home and discarded the thing in the dumpster, a police car pulled to an abrupt halt in front of me. The officer called out. I approached the car, unconcerned. He investigated me, questioning me about the cat. I asked if someone had called the police. Someone had. I laughed. The situation diffused itself, since I was clearly no threat. Though the officer gave me a confused look, he returned to his car and drove off, no crime having been committed. I collected myself and disappeared once more indoors. But it serves as an example of how removed from the world I was becoming.

I went away to be alone, practiced my earliest meditations, wrote in journals, sought novel experiences, and the rest that a young solitary person might try, a whole slew of experiments, and very quickly my sense of propriety vanished, leaving me quite oblivious to the expectations of others and odder than ever. I wandered the streets alone, and if someone approached me, I promptly left them where they stood and walked away. As much as possible, I pretended the ordinary world didn't exist, keeping myself obscured behind tree-lined paths during the day or venturing into uninhabited places all night. I felt more and more removed from others, drifting off into my own world, looking for strange places from which I could study the moon, and dark places from which I could view the overarching twilight. People eyed me with suspicion when I came out of alleyways, paused on the sidewalk in the middle of the night with my head staring at the stars, or stood too long in the rain.

Time passed. I became more independent, but the experiences I had with people tended more and more to drag me down. I suppose those who were rude were in their own private hells. But I did come across quite a bit of hostility for no satisfactory reason. Once, I staggered about in a paint store, lingering too long at a shelf of acrylic paints. My mind was a blank. I hardly knew where I was, so tired was I from a long walk all night. The sun had been up for hours but I had yet to sleep, so my mind was fragmented, a tired distance from everything around me. An employee eventually threw me out because it looked as if I were either attempting to steal or prepared to cause trouble. "What are you doing?" he greeted me. I was haggard, worn, dangerous-looking. I told him I was looking at the paints. "Get out," he said. I was shocked by his hostility. It left me feeling disturbed and disturbing. The responses I inspired in those days tended to be like that: I was veering into exile.

I loved the moon, the sunsets, the mountains that lay every-where in the dark. One night in a field alongside a dirt road, I stopped to watch the twilight, and after the sun went down, the western horizon became purplish. From the horizon, the purple spread over the sky with a transparent glow, light then darkening layer by layer. The darkness of the night grew upward from the other side of the sky, and the darkness and the purple met in the middle for a moment before the night overcame it. Then a deep black settled over everything. I stood alone in the middle of nowhere, having embarked to some outer edge of existence.

I'd been roaming for hours. My eyes quickly adjusted to the night and I went on into the grayness, up over the steep hillsides to linger about beneath a dark tree atop them. Across the mountains that lay everywhere in the dark, I saw meadows go on like oceans, with a gray textured look as if night itself were a substance laid down upon them. A vast landscape stretched unpopulated for miles, draped in darkness. It suggested loneliness, like loneliness itself had made its home there. I felt a kinship with it. It reflected my feelings exactly. The dejection in me was alive in the night, the trees were tangled in it, their black branches blending with the darkness. The wind that blew, an exhilarating wind, though cold and forbidding, gave the darkness a somber character, like the strange places of the world, old temples seen at dusk and miles and miles of shipless seas at night.

While I was in the midst of the wilds of the world, the city went on as usual. As I grew more and more detached from the ordinary world, people became strange. More often in those days, they were unpleasant, angry, and brutish. Sensitivity wasn't a marked trait in anyone I encountered. While I went off alone, the troubles of life didn't change. The same old television lights flickered in every house. The news reports went on with all the violence they had always gone on with: murders, kidnappings, beatings, bombings, as if the world were at war with itself at all hours of the day, people against people, hostilities in the streets and between countries. People woke, ate breakfast, drove to work, worked all day, then went home to sit in front of their televisions, exhausted and apathetic, before sleeping till the next day, at which time the same would be repeated. When I saw them, they appeared numb, showing every sign of submission to powerlessness, and intensely angry without knowing the reason; confused, desensitized, hardened. For my part, I searched for a private path, a different limb of the tree, because nothing much else appealed to me but the hidden and the interior.

5

But this is not an autobiography. Not in the ordinary sense. Instead, it's the equivalent of, more or less, a thought autobiography, a free examination of my thoughts and their role in my life. It's a light shed erratically on what's inside me, finally, after all I've experienced, at least at this stage of my life. Whereas an autobiography would detail my lunatic nights and my crazed moments of eerie delusion, as well as the acute misery of my childhood, in this case a simple sketch of my life will do. All things considered, this is not an account of what led me to where I am, but rather an account of the thoughts that arose as a result of arriving where I am, who I am because of what I think. My life did indeed go on into strangeness, unpleasantness, suffering, quiet rage, love lulled to dullness, exasperation. I remember being disturbed more often than enchanted by life.

It seems that more often than not the defiant are simply defeated by life, replaced by those more able to deal with the depression, the nihilism that inevitably comes, the lack of tenderness in everyday interactions on the street. The easy-going have it better than the oversensitive. When a door slams too hard I feel threatened. I like things soft. Delicate. I'm relieved by silence. I feel as if life has beaten me to a pulp and now I'm frightened of the next blow. I've been hungry before, sad before, lonely before. I've been hysterical with suicidal impulses, and I've been homesick for times in my life when things were better.

I know what it feels like to feel inadequate. For a great many years, I believed myself inept, inferior, unlovable. I wonder if everyone goes through that? That period where it feels as if nobody could possibly love you, nobody ever will, and nothing is ever going to change or be all right. I loathed those days. So much more because I broke again and again, just struggling, holding on, but barely, sick of holding on.

I'd cure myself with a long walk. I'd become enamored by the sunlight through the trees, the leaves a bright yellow like they were made of light. I'd walk for miles alone along hidden paths, deep into the woods or high up into the mountains, for so many hours that the stars would come out and speckle the sky like tiny eyes looking down upon me from other worlds.

Something about the complex systems of society and the institutions that oversaw everything seemed inherently to reject me. Accordingly, it appeared that I wasn't made to be in existence. Thus, whatever life offered, I only felt good when alone. I couldn't find my place on earth except when alone.

Without existing friendships, my life was bizarre, vanishing into some perpetual absence separate from the rest of the world. When the world was deserted, without people, being in it was far more comfortable. Throughout the night, I sat alone beneath the trees, played under wet branches, lay in the dirt and watched the stars, found the moon reflected in bare black water. The sensation of being alone under the stars, the moon, the swaying trees on some mountain overlooking the valleys below was that of being home. During the prime of my life, I stood atop the heights of precarious cliffs, the sharp ledges beneath the tips of my feet. The outermost hinterland was all around me, and I searched for something invisible to the ordinary world. Out there, beneath the night sky, having left the ordinary world behind, the human condition was silly: billions and billions of stars lit up distances that ridiculed the petty conflicts on earth.

One of those daily word vocabulary-building calendars was on my refrigerator. The word "joviality" was on it. It's a decent word. I learned it, however, in the darkest period of my life, when the least thing I felt was happiness. At the time, I was too young to be disillusioned; I was rather disliked. I felt disliked. It seemed that each time I ventured out into the world I encountered people who had it in for me. I'm not sure why. It came on like a curse. Surrounding me was a black aura that invited hostility. My luck was bad. My initial steps into the world were greeted by abuse. Maybe I didn't play the right game: knocking horns together, sparring with words, penis jousting. Nevertheless, the case was clear. Mistreatment caused pain. When it went on and on it intensified my natural depression, and my introverted social habit became a philosophy. Sometimes it roused a bitter, long-lasting revulsion for people in general. I felt disliked, and so I began to dislike.

The reason I felt disliked was clear: I found myself continually subjected to hostility. However, I'm unsure what brought on that hostility. I wasn't mean-looking, yet my brows did have a twist of despair set into them. The right side was held up while the left was held low, sculpted in that fashion by prolonged misery. Mine was the face of anguish. It's quite possible that the expression of unhappiness on my face provided an open invitation to hostility, most specifically from those compelled to add to the suffering of the already weakened.

People seem to pit themselves against each other out of habit. It goes on like a circular rhythm. One is hostile, making the next hostile. It's passed from person to person in the air. It's a cycle the world lives in, hostility and hate and fear and pain traveling from person to person like a contagion. It ruins most everything. It wears down on the innocent until they change, become colder to survive. A hardness is needed to get through the day. Sensitivity is given up and replaced with a necessary desensitization. Every moment somewhere on earth, like the seasons, the cycle is renewed. It comes and goes, but it's always somewhere in one hemisphere or another. Eventually, it's decided that nobody cares. Nobody cares about me. Nobody really wants me. Nobody's going to be there for me.

So many people in the modern world are so angry. They're stripped of everything when quite young and given nonsense in return, trinkets hardly worth living for. The greater part of the world has become a system without pride led by greed. Not joviality. What I see in my neighborhood are haggard people who walk the streets with bottles of alcohol to numb the pain. They collapse at home on their threadbare couches. Their hands hang off the edges of the couches, off the edge of the world like suicides.

Half the people I've seen are visibly disgusted, dismal, distressed, disheveled because they no longer care. Something beat life out of them, and it's been a long time coming. Young men without the energy to get out of bed lie about unshaven. Young women who don't know what to make of things grow tired. Abysmal lives just go on and on. Eventually, some of them become belligerent bastards: angry, mean, rotten, rude, ruthless, sad, savage, unwanted people.

The monstrous thing is that it's so difficult to love. With fear everywhere, fear in people's hearts and minds, showing love is almost like risking your neck. People are more afraid to show each other how much they care than they are to throw up their hands, give up, and do the easy thing, which is to be deplorable to each other. People will be rude before they show love, because it's easier.

Life is unsatisfactory. There's too much nonsense to sort through. Before enough of it is figured out, enough damage has been done to cause the repetition of the cycle. Looking into someone's eyes with a heart full of love is terrifying. Instead, wary eyes are everywhere. Admirable personality traits don't include wide-open arms, loving people on the street, or giving hugs to strangers crying on the bus. People are suspicious of each other, strangers might be criminals, and nobody can be trusted. People have a bad reputation.

It serves the whole mess. It serves it perfectly well, if the mess is to be kept. But in my mind, a billion or more people on earth want to give someone a hug, tell a person they care, and do what they can. But they can't. Something doesn't allow it. The result is haggard and hostile people who drown away their sufferings in hidden rooms until they've broken. At least, I've seen enough of that. The most wicked louse was likely fresh and pure at one point in time. Now menacing. Hurt, broken, now menacing. A person's face becomes ugly after too many beatings, and so does the heart.

There's only so much it can take before it breaks. An openhearted smile on everyone's face, flashed to every stranger, would be ideal, but the distinct feature of walking down a public street is a dismal sadness, a dissociated estrangement from every other person. In public, the city streets might as well be underneath a downpour of rain. People generally look downward, at their feet, rather than into the eyes of passersby. Words are seldom used. Strangers remain strangers. To transcend this mundane situation, a few people do daring things like stand on street corners and offer free hugs. Because those are met with acceptance, I wonder: If civilization removed all the posturing, would it be in love with everyone at all times? Nirvana on every street. The most intimate companionship from complete strangers. Unconditional love given away for nothing.

The fact is that when fear is there, love is eclipsed. It isn't fear that people desire, however, but to love. Art shows this constantly. If people didn't desire to give and to receive love so much, the world wouldn't be filled with so much creative counsel in its favor. At the end of the day, benevolent dispositions are everywhere hidden behind frowns and frustrated faces. There's rank, superiority and inferiority, good and evil, self-doubt, tongue-tied anxiety, constantly disheartened moods, status, the rich and the poor, disgust and hate, countries at war, and always those stupid bombs that are built. It makes a bad impression. The cycle persists as much from the silence as from the noise. As my life went, I was at peace when alone. This because each time I wandered out into the world I was met with hostility. I already felt inadequate and awkward enough.

6

As an adolescent, I was suicidal quite often, with little care for my safety. I liked to sleep because it afforded me the opportunity to avoid living. But when I couldn't sleep, I'd escape the suicidal impulse by trekking into the mountains, though partially hoping to encounter a wild animal, vicious, hungry, devouring. In my imagination, I'd meet a wolf hidden in the dark amidst the trees; a dirty, starved creature. It would leap upon me and kill me. I wouldn't resist. Thus my need to endure life would come to an end, at least in a more natural way than suicide, and in a way, I'd be grateful for it.

Hence, I feared nothing out there. All night I'd ascend a gravel trail that went up into the wilds. The window of a run-down farmhouse would float by in the night, with its dim light glowing in the dark, as I passed beyond it and into no-man's-land.

One night on this trail, as unlikely as it seems, I became the inspiration for a ghost story. I might have looked odd in my gray raincoat. But it was my general pallor, my white skin and unusually white hair, that likely made me look ghostly in the dark.

As was my custom during my walks, I gazed about myself at the sights until I lost my sense of self. I passed a line of trees, the same old trees that were always gray and forbidding with shadows, and I was out there, out beyond. The moon was covered. It was dark. The clouds filled the sky with torn sheets of purple, concealing even the stars. I trekked along and tired myself until I was gnawed on by fatigue. But I pressed on anyway, step after step. I was pale in the dark, aglow with sweat, gravitating toward something surreal.

I haunted those mountains. I wandered all night into the middle of nowhere, deep into the uninviting outermost reaches, until I was numb. When the sunrise came, I was atop the highest peak. I stood and watched. The sun came up with yellowish fingers in the clouds. Then, after it was over, I descended the mountain almost too preoccupied with my experience to notice a man passing by me.

He stared at me strangely, but he didn't say a word. I glanced at him out of the corner of my eye to take him in. The expression on his face was aghast. He was drawn back, with wide eyes fixed in alarm, jaw slightly open, eyebrows taut with confusion. I was as white as a ghost, the blood vessels having retreated from my skin due to the cold. I was wild in the face from the sight of the sunrise. And he looked hunted when I came near.

I passed him wordlessly, more or less indifferently in fact. I was too adrift in my night of wandering to notice much of the mundane world around me. But a while later, the night over, the world and the earth resumed their daily routine. For me, life returned to normal. I found myself walking in the morning light down the gravel road that led back home. Nothing remained as ethereal as the night. I felt completely natural. Things were perfectly ordinary to me. Things weren't remarkable or strange. I saw the dawn rising just as it did on any other day. My senses became more wakeful and less dreamy as the daylight brightened, and my face flushed with color once again. But I hadn't the faintest suspicion of how strange I must have appeared all the while I had been up there alone in the dark.

Around that time, a legend began. It was said that a young boy could be seen at night wandering the mountains, a young boy who haunted the landscape, a young ghostly boy matching my description. He wore a gray raincoat, he had white skin and unusually white hair, and he was seen to perambulate the mountains all night. When in fact all I'd wished to do was escape, because I lived more intensely on the mountaintops, striding from peak to peak, wandering in the dark, losing myself in the open air, I'd become a ghost. Years later, I read about myself in a journal of ghostly encounters in the region. Evidently the impression I'd made was unusual.

7

It seems to have been fifty or one hundred years, or longer still – a thousand, ten thousand.

At one point, I enrolled in a few courses at a local college. I was motivated by my dream, by the long-fingered scholars who sought the meaning of life. It was a whimsical decision. I'd likely been in a good mood, a more fearless mood, when I'd made it. However, I should have reconsidered. During the enrollment process, I was plunged into a crowd of students. It took incredible effort for me to remain in the crowd. By the time I had to have a photograph taken of me, my nerves were overwrought and I looked into the camera with a shocked expression. The photographer had to stop for a moment. Before she snapped the picture, she said, "Don't look so scared."

My condition was worsening. It had been a rapid decline. College turned out to be intolerable. On an afternoon when I was idling after classes, a girl approached me on the steps where I sat. She stopped, concerned, and asked, "Are you okay?" I was terrified of the other students. Their easy self-assurance was enviable, yet for me it succeeded only in highlighting my shyness. I stiffened at her voice, nodded with a jerk, and murmured, "Yes, I'm okay. I'm just tired." But that wasn't it. My face was visibly sick, gaunt and haggard. It felt like a stone weighed down by desperation. All day, I'd gone from classroom to classroom. My gaze had wandered away from strangers, anywhere but their faces. I'd walked on alone through crowds with my head down. In the halls, I'd caught the eye of a young woman, but I'd averted my eyes in shame, like a starving man without a mouth.

When the semester was finally over and my theater class had come to an end, for the final goodbye the class went to see a play. The play was by an unremembered playwright from around the time of Shakespeare. It could have been mistaken for one of Shakespeare's plays. A man fell in love with a woman, which was the main spectacle. There were love scenes and articulate words. A second pair, clownish, also fell in love, which provided comedy relief. I didn't care much for any of it.

What I did find exciting, however, was looking into the faces of the actors. I was able to admire them in secret, from the darkness, and stare directly into their eyes. The only light, the stage light, was on them, and their eyes were spectacular, glistening in it. As I stared on, I was communicating or falling in love.

Sometimes they faced me, and my experience intensified as a result. Their romantic speeches might have been directed at me. And for hours it went on. Desire.

When the play was over and we prepared to depart, the other students waited about in the courtyard. An afterparty. I could not have been more nervous. And I choked. I felt nearly frozen in the corner. Even at the end of the semester, I had no idea how to make friends. The others struck up conversations while I stood alone, oppressed by shyness. It began to rain. I lost myself in the leaves of a nearby plant, in the rain on its leaves. Nobody approached me. To my relief, the professor finally came to tell us to load onto the bus. But by the time it was over, I'd been through a great ordeal. I felt feeble.

I had to deal with my fate, though it was certainly not appealing for me to consider where that fate might lead. I knew full well that I had no need to endure my suffering any longer than I wished to endure it. My thoughts of suicide had only intensified during that semester of college. Altogether, I approached life as if on my way into exile, as if all the doors that might return me to amicable civilization were closed.

It was for this reason that I found myself standing late at night in the middle of the street, peering into the windows of strange houses. I was fascinated by the hovering yellow lights of bedroom windows and kitchens and places where families gathered. Somehow the light itself seemed warm. A tender benevolence seemed to come from those homes. Soft and pleasant. It was the feeling of being beside a fire: a home filled with calm, and love between the faces of the wife and husband.

I remember stopping at a bridge quite often during my walks. The path to the bridge was hidden beneath trees and the whole scene was quite forbidding at night. Two yellow lights gleamed dimly from two black poles at both sides of the bridge. No other light could be seen. It reminded me of an eerie chiaroscuro, like one of Rembrandt's paintings: a ghostly glow in the darkness, reminiscent of a place one would go to make a secret deal, or a place one would go to remain unknown. I was always there alone, and it was always late.

My hand would brush the bridge's splintered handrail as I walked across, and in the yellow light, the scene was always vivid. It was late fall, and the rain would come. The leaves would crackle; the familiar odor of wet earth would rise from the soil like a perfume. I'd follow the path out of the darkness and stop at the houses. I'd look up into the little yellow windows, and I'd feel overwhelmed by loneliness. Other people belonged to the world. It was no trivial feeling. I was exiled.

The worst feeling a human being can endure is to feel unlovable. The outcome is a madman. He'll feel bitter toward what's lovely. He'll spit curses at the beauty of a rose. He'll rail against the sky. He'll lie in bed at night cursing himself. All of this goes on, and on. And somewhere, there it is. Imagine all the hostility in the world that's been born from the same wound.

8

I declined further. Just as I suspected I would. By the time I lived alone, my method of self-extermination was to stay drunk and chain smoke, crumpled beneath the covers of my bed, refusing to let the sun into my room. My constant companion was a nihilistic mood, the feeling that there was no value or use in living, nor in seeking a better life. Slow suicide. Alcohol, cigarettes, and depression in a bed covered by a subtle death shroud. The closeness of suicide was nearer and nearer. It became my custom to linger about with an inescapable ache, an unnatural torpor, the cacophony of real life happening somewhere outside my window while I watched my life explode with misery. Something crept into me: a deep, black, desolate dark.

Sometimes I think the only thing keeping people alive is the fear of death. The pain of life is too often too much, but there remains the terrible fear of dying. If life and death were determined by a light switch, one that could simply be flicked off, without pain, without terror, I suspect there would be a great number of people making their escape.

I drank too much. I shuffled back and forth in my room, hateful. In the middle of the day, I lay in bed awake, wishing I wasn't awake. More often than not, I simply stayed in bed. If I slept, I woke from fitful dreams. When I couldn't sleep, I drank more, until my room was a museum of various empty alcohol bottles.

Several dark bottles rested on the windowsill of my room like decorative trinkets. Among the books scattered on the floor were old cigarette butts. I wore the same unwashed clothes day in and day out. My hair was wild and oily, sticking up in all directions. My face had a gray look and a tired expression. Each morning, looking into the bathroom mirror, I noticed how my features grew more and more phantasmal. I was sick with the struggle within me. Life was wrong. A murderous war. And everything was a bombed-out church.

In my room, flowers were spread thickly on my desk: dead flowers from the numerous weddings held at the hotel where I worked. I'd become morbidly obsessed with the weddings, and I collected the leftover flowers, dried into hard little stems with pieces of the petals here and there, some of the petals still holding onto the eye of the flower while others lay in disarray, strewn everywhere: pink, red, white roses. My room looked like the decimated remains of a wedding ceremony.

I was sick, but I didn't care. I was sick with the exhaustion of apathy. The world was absurd and carried on indifferent to humanity.

I dreamt one night that I was living outdoors, homeless, and the park in which I slept had had an office complex built over the top of it during the night. I awoke in the dream lying in the dirt underneath the foundation, buried alive, so to speak. I saw, through the cracks in the construction, people going about their business, buying things, selling things, without knowing I was down there underneath it all. The world went on built right over me.

There was a man living near me with whom I became briefly acquainted, a neighbor of mine who was in love with the Queen of England. He could be seen at night outside his room, during the latest hours, with spit falling from his mouth and his swaying hand holding an empty bottle of whiskey. Each night, he stood outside and drifted off into unconsciousness. When I saw him, all I thought about was the woman he must have loved. He lived alone. He was happy, in a way, drinking himself into a stupor night after night. That was the reality of things: his grubby hands holding a bottle, the drool coming from his lips, the numbing of the pain. He had that sort of despair lingering about him that speaks of love. His eyes were soft, his face was gentle, but his hands would tremble. His great love was not the Queen of

England. However, she must have been someone. And I saw myself there, in that lost gaze in his eyes when he was all but gone. I supposed that I was the same. Night after night, I drank myself to sleep, and I'd stopped reaching for anything better.

9

But let me get to the point. My life had been continuing in the described fashion for quite some time. I'd developed a ghostlike nature. I'd become an apparition. The cities and the streets had faded into a world for other people, not me. Eventually, however, and because of all this, my thoughts had changed, sometimes ascending and sometimes descending, but ultimately seeking with vigilance for some measurable purpose to my life, until one night I arrived in the landscape of the surreal.

My thoughts over the course of four days, which arose in a fever of delirium, irrevocably changed my life. I was transformed.

I'd rather not attempt to explain the impossible. Or pour the impossible onto the page. Instead, I'd like to exercise restraint. I'd like all this to have been perfectly ordinary, but in fact it was not.

Using words, I'd taken an antagonistic position toward myself. In the midst of a self-critical review of my psyche, as I'm doing now, something new had come into view. The experiment had reached its conclusion. It was over.

I no longer existed. I was free. I can't describe what that's like.

Each person must find their own unique solution to the problem of being. A completely different person must find a completely individual answer. If it were possible to find an answer for everyone, someone would already have written the solution to the suffering in the world. There's a great deal of suffering. Certainly there's been a great deal of talk about it. But the solution remains indistinct, remote, a Rorschach inkblot with several stains upon it, a cigarette burn, the smear of blood from someone's bleeding finger.

My mind was unshackled. It became unhinged. It was the origination of all that's come since. I've been spiraling unseen in my mind, living in an interior universe, evolving in my unconscious, my shadow self brought into the light. But I'm uncertain how to describe it. Which is closer to the truth: the reality into which I was born or the reality that came after my insanity?

The lunacy lasted for days and nights on end. I didn't sleep. I lay in bed gripped by visions. Everything began. Nights more unusual than any before. What can the eyes tell of reality? What does an optic nerve see except a mere particle of something far more magnificent that's the undercurrent of all that's before the eyes?

Every day for four days, I'd been in my room. I was in an altered state of mind, caused by insomnia and an unintended fast. I'd created a schism in my being, stepped aside from myself until my body was a foreign entity, and looking at it I'd discovered that all its actions were those of an automaton.

My room became disjointed. It was crumbling around me, disintegrating at the level of its atomic structure. I could hardly understand anything in existence, much less my perception of reality. I'd abandoned myself, unloosened my mind so as to root out the deeper, learned, habitual behaviors and therefore be free, at least to some degree, and after gazing upon myself for days, my eyes had found the truth of what I was with the blinders of self-deception removed.

Pandora's box sprang open. Inside were a thousand shimmering nightmares. Whatever had happened before those days had been a dream lived by someone else. In bed, I felt a tumultuous rush of emotions shoot through me. First, I was overcome by intense fear, as if I'd seen the personification of my fear, but the feeling was physical only. It had no mental qualities. It was caused by no thought. There was no cause. My thoughts were calm, unafraid, and I lay in bed as if bearing witness, cool-headed, comfortable, while my body felt as if it had seen a ghoul and was, for hours, gripped by fear.

Next came shame. Then anger. Shame came on with a burning in the center of my chest, a slightly hollow feeling, and my face flushed and grew hot. Anger came on with a tension in my temples and heavier breathing, even though there was nothing to be angry about. It went on. And on. I felt the full range of human emotions, one after the other, hour after hour, for four days, feelings without a conscious cause. It was an onslaught. The bliss was like radiant angels. The terror was like unimaginably horrifying deities. But I felt only the physiological response. Mentally, I experienced no fear, no shame, no anger.

I lay in bed and watched. I recognized the automatism, the reflexive, habitual nature of my emotions. Their biology. They were the undercurrent of my conscious life, sometimes frightful, sometimes terrible, but they belonged only to the body that for hours I'd been detachedly observing. They belonged to a stranger with my name. All the wringing of my hands and the despondence of my emotional life had arisen from just such feelings. But they went on automatically just then. And it was liberating – the knowledge that my emotions could have no justifying cause and yet feel exactly the same. I experienced a whole slew of emotions without mental attachment to them. Later, I rose from the experience as if from mesmerism, my mind illuminated and the whole exquisite world alive in my senses.

I felt my being rise to the surface. It was as if the breath of life had ascended from the bottom of a murky sea. My being was distinctly enraptured, a joy a thousand times stronger than the first feeling I had as a child. My capacity for rationality, however, seemed to be gone. I hardly knew how many nights had passed since I'd last slept. I'd vanished. I was nonexistent and an amnesiac. My remembered self no longer belonged to me. I was no longer him or his absurdity, but had dissociated, like a mirror broke and nobody stood before it and that was the real truth of things.

My emotional life and emotional understanding of everything around me was missing from my thoughts. So I sat in the moment, observing myself, just some essence that remained, the being. Who had I been? I'd been thoughts, emotions, reactions that circled through my mind habitually as a result of its conditioning. I saw that clearly, that what I'd believed to have been myself had been an endless cycle, spanning the length of my life. I'd reacted to situations again and again in the same way. I'd thought and felt and even known things. But they made no sense except to that mind trapped in a cycle. Without emotion, I was no longer me. The self and its identity were false. They were Pavlov's dog salivating automatically at the sound of a bell. Conditioned responses to a world made of conditioning stimuli.

For days in my room, I went through this drama. I felt bliss. One moment, I felt the eradication of pain, the next fear, then horror. I felt terror. My body was spiraling with emotion, cyclical, illusory, false, but my mind was unknown, unformed, a fog in the morning disappearing into the sky, a dream. It was beautiful and frightening. And throughout the experience an unassailable being rested within me.

I had no other sense of who I was but this expression of being. The history of my life had been a set of dominoes knocking one another down, one moment having led to the next with a destined reaction in a long line of events, a chain reaction, that had led me to believe things, view things, experience things, and feel things in a certain way, and I'd believed all of it to have been myself.

Reaction. What had my life been but that?

For four days, I was insane. Nothing made sense. The patterns of my mind that had been kept neatly organized had been thrown down on the floor like a game swept aside. I couldn't point to anything physical as me: my hand floating in the air beside me, hanging slightly, reaching for my cup of coffee, fumbling with an unopened pack of cigarettes, reaching for the bottle of whiskey in my desk drawer. I saw myself from a distance, and all of what I saw myself doing belonged to someone else. My actions were rehearsed actions. They were a cycling of consciousness, as if I were a machine designed to manufacture something as banal as bolts. Habits. My brain moved with images, scraps of life and memory, scenes, but the coming of these images was habitual, the working of a dull machine. From the perspective of distance, they were hallucinations, illusions, falsities. My real self for the length of those four days was my being, which was nothing. It was unconditioned, a pinpoint adrift in the eye of the storm, alive like a single-celled macrocosm.

My symbols had disappeared. It was that mind-altering. I found no representations of my thoughts, no words in my vocabulary because words carried no weight. I was fully aware that they had once contained meaning, but their meanings became connotations, shades of prejudice, liking and disliking. Without emotion, every word was wiped of these. Their associations were absurd. To say that a book was a book was no longer accurate, because a book came with a whole slew of associated meanings that no longer existed. Because the self that had felt emotional attachments to words was gone, words became meaningless. No attachments, no shades of meaning, no connotations: it was staggering how much of my language was built by them.

I was in that room for one hundred years. A century hovered lethargically in the light. The dust was sedimentary. I relaxed and let go. Then my muscles became rigid and I bolted out of bed. Mania and madness. At twelve midnight I was raving mad. At sunrise it hadn't stopped. A breakdown was inevitable. It finally ended with a long sleep, over twenty hours. When I awoke, I was new with madness, a changed brain. It was liberation aided by insanity. The conditioned constructs of my mind, my mental history, my autobiographical emotional landscape had been freed of all past meaning, and I spent some time in bliss, the very same bliss I had experienced when looking at the stars as a child, experiencing the unconditioned being.

10

At this stage of my life, after all my wanderings, after learning from the night skies and the dark fields, I could find peace of mind even in rags. I'd slip into rags as if they were a lavish robe. Live a life of luxurious poverty. I don't need much or want much. My experience of the interior has left me disinterested in ordinary things. When with others, I'd rather be with their interiors.

I've been a spiritual vagabond. It's always been an attractive lifestyle choice to me, idling languidly without desire, living the life of a free tramp, a wanderer through the cities, a lost dreamer after years of dreaming. I've spent my nights under the moon, a bottle of wine in hand, drunk outdoors as it should be, the whole world awaiting a lifetime of tramping over it, nobody remembering my name. I'd not mind living under bridges in cities and along the roadsides, sleeping in wild fields alone beneath the sky and the opulence of stars at night.

It depends on the perspective taken toward poverty. It might be one of romanticism, as it is with me. I don't have any money, nor do I care to have any. I don't have need for much. It's a choice that comes with a certain freedom. I have free time, and that provides a chance to learn all day. I learn from the flowers. I've received my education from the overgrown forests, from the great mountains, from the unpopulated, remote worlds discovered when alone.

Old baubles and trinkets have never had appeal to me. My possessions amount to a stack of books that would fill a suitcase, a few sets of clothes, a pair of boots, and a coffee brewer. I'd even prefer less, the penniless life of a bird. It owns nothing and takes its sustenance freely from the fields. Its inheritance is simplicity. Yet, its world is vast.

11

On an ordinary night, I walked through the city. I was wandering in and out of alleyways, up and down the streets. In the dark, the city was in solitude, a deserted paradise of buildings and sidewalks, vivid in the streetlights, unreal and unpopulated. I was the only member of the human race on the streets that night, a ghost perambulating about in an empty world, unseen.

I came across an all-night coffee shop, brightly lit up. A young man was sitting by himself inside, staring forward, sipping coffee, lost in thought. When the little bell on the door jingled as I went in, he watched me. I ordered the cheapest coffee and sat down. He approached me, friendly, oblivious to my oddness at first, likely not expecting me to be any different from another patron of the coffee shop. He asked me if I'd like to play chess.

We took a chess board outside and sat at a table. Just then the wind picked up, and by the time we had our pieces arranged, the wind whipped them down, scattering them everywhere. But he protested when I suggested we move inside. When we managed to fix the pieces, I moved mine with the trembling hand of a shy recluse. He tried to make conversation, but to every question he asked me, I replied in a cracked voice. I couldn't escape the feeling that I was making a bad impression.

He was slightly older than me and I determined he was a student. Whereas my speech was quite inarticulate, his was quite sophisticated. I managed to ask him about his life, and indeed he was a student, a recuperating university student. He then spoke on and on with ease about his studies. He was very intelligent, an introspective sort with a wide array of experience and book learning, someone with very little self-doubt.

He was at the coffee shop waiting for friends, and when they arrived, though perhaps it was only in my imagination, he seemed eager to escape my company. The group was a flashy sort, in their prime. They were likely his friends from the university. The young man went outside to greet them, then returned for a moment, as if prepared to invite me along. But he changed his mind. He closed the door. I was alone again, and felt I'd done poorly. The chance at friendship was lost, and a sense of deficiency came over me. I felt inept. I left the coffee shop and wandered through the streets, lightening my mood by directing my attention upward to the moon. It was full just then, a pale, pearly thing in the blackness, and it managed to eliminate my despondence by filling me with wonder.

12

When I was younger, about fifteen years old, I decided to go off alone and search for the remote places of the world. While the cities built skyscrapers and had streets full of automobiles, I sought out lonesome mountains and hidden riversides. I wanted to find solitude. I wanted to search myself in the solitary landscapes. Because something was wrong. Precisely what was wrong was indefinite. My moods were dark. I was full of halting and hesitant speech. My custom was to bungle about in life in the habit of self-condemnation. I didn't belong to the modern world or its people. This was made clear each time I was jarred by the busy streets. A shock of fear overcame me when I was out in them. On the street, I felt fragile. I was overly frail and oversensitive by nature, I suppose. As I walked in public, I shifted my eyes down, away from strangers, onto my boots. Whenever possible, I avoided conversation. I avoided any interaction whatsoever. I ducked away. Silently. Wordlessly. It was a rare occasion when I spoke aloud. Introspection was the natural result. My inclination was to avoid everything in life and bury myself inward. I felt far more peaceful when I focused on my interior. It was less obnoxious than the clamor of life in the streets. It was more comfortable to leave the surface world and all it had to offer, to vanish, to lose myself in fantasies, to escape inside.

During the years that I managed to stay in school, which weren't very many at all, a tongue-tied horror took hold of me. The stress was too much. I walked the grounds stiffly, as polite as possible but reserved, expressing nothing of the cheer of my peers. I was startled by the extent of my inhibition when I was near people. I felt benevolence for them, desired their companionship, and was even offered companionship on several occasions. Still, I ran off to be alone. Whenever someone was near, I managed to drift into absent-mindedness, especially on the occasions when I was directly addressed. It provided escape. I spent my time wandering about lost in my inward landscape in order to lessen my cognizance of being in public. The fear of it. And I made every effort to be as lost as possible. I loathed being in public. I loathed the hideousness of my fear of it. The whole thing was abhorrent. Even if my classmates were cheerful and pleasant enough, benevolent and warm, I stammered my speech and babbled distracted nonsense to them when addressed, then looked immediately for a means to escape. I felt sick. By the end of the day, my frayed nerves were quite uncomfortable, and the years were terrible as a result.

My situation was that, at home, awaiting me, a hypercritical, bad-tempered middle-aged man, my father, was hostile toward my every movement. Through the years, a sense of danger, of being afraid, had shifted onto everything, as such a thing does. It had seeped into everything else, giving it a bad character. Without my being aware of the transference, I'd projected my homelife onto the whole world. Eventually, being disliked at home, I felt disliked by everyone. It was a habit, something I'd grown accustomed to, and my manner reflected it. Gradually, I took on the mannerisms of someone intensely uncomfortable: nervous, diminished, half a person, half a shadow. My eyes looked downward because I felt glaring sneers when in public, even at the times when there were none. The whole thing weakened me, and moreover, tended to invite hostilities, as such a thing does. I was psychologically exhausted. I needed relief, and so I found it in places where nobody went, places where I could be alone.

There was a photograph taken of me when I was young. It was definitive of the condition of my life. In the photograph, my eyes were enlarged as if on the verge of terror, my eyebrows were contorted, consistent with the grief I felt, and my lips, which made a concerted effort to smile, conveyed rather than a smile the misery of a whimper. To add to the effect of the photograph, the pallor of my face produced the overall appearance of someone sickly, eerily white. It was a strange and terrified look I gave the photographer. All things considered, it was the face of someone who had deteriorated far too much: a monstrous discomfort weighed upon that miserable face.

I wasn't the durable sort. I was delicate by nature, one of the more fragile in society. I was growing into adulthood, but I nevertheless feared the thought of adult life. Convinced I'd be incapable of making my own way in the world, an idea I'd learned, unpleasantly, from my childhood years, I was assured by every thought in every corner of my mind that I was inept and unfit for living. It was easy for me to slip into comparisons of myself with others and find myself continually falling short. In essence, I'd been condemned enough to begin to condemn myself. I believed that I was condemned, with nothing in my future but to live out the life of a withdrawn specter.

To my mind, my future would be spent trying unsuccessfully to arrive at happiness. Instead of finding it, I'd be preoccupied for the length of my life by fears. I'd be hampered by inhibition. I'd slump into my chair night after night feeling little but rejection. Finally, after a lifetime of seeking relief from the malaise of my nervous temperament, I'd find death had arrived, with nothing much having changed in my life. I feared I'd come to an end before I'd find freedom from any of it.

I was able to go off on my own. Partly, it was skepticism that led me to leave. I sought a more endurable world, a world less directed by harshness. I imagined myself wandering the mountainsides looking for a better existence. By the time I'd find myself in that strange locale between light and darkness, with the orange cast coming over the sky when the sun would begin to set, the moon becoming visible on the horizon, the first stars beginning to come out, I'd be gone, lost in some other world completely apart from the ordinary.

I left the ordinary world. I searched myself in the solitary landscapes, in the quiet, in the stillness. I'd brush my fingers against the uncritical leaves of bushes and trees to touch nonjudgmental nature. I enjoyed spending my time in solitude because it was transforming. When alone in the remote places of the world, it's natural for the mystical to show itself, because solitude is mysterious, strange. The world begins to fall away and reveal a magical oddity, something beneath, something that inspires soul searching and seeking for answers, a divine vein with an immaterial essence more startling and alive than anything on the surface.

The woods, the mountains, and the distant landscapes served as the perfect locations to lose myself and find what was inside. My tight neck and constricted nerves loosened up, and the burden of my morbid depressions was replaced by a passion for the otherworldly. When nobody was around, my being unfurled. I was inspired. All night amidst the meadows, the moonlight making them luminous, I saw through the mundane and looked delightedly into the eerie. My body felt lighter than a living body, and I transformed into something imperceptible, a mirage beneath the moon, something odd that belonged nowhere but within. I found another self, the drifting being, insubstantial but growing.

13

I spent many years alone, in a cheap little apartment at the edge of the city. It became habitual for me to linger about in isolated worlds removed from the bustle of the streets. Rather quickly, I lost my need to belong to the world. I found acceptance in the landscapes and the wilderness, which had no judgments to make, presented no obstacles to my enjoying them, inspired no fear, filled my senses and calmed my emotions. I contemplated the cells in flowers until an uncanny feeling washed over me, a sense of the mysterious, a feeling that life possessed a distinctly miraculous majesty beneath the whole of the universe. In everything around me, I sensed an inner being, and it filled me with an unreserved reverence.

During the years I spent alone, the change started small, a slight sensation as fleetingly noticed as a heartbeat. But it grew rapidly. The likeness of an internal entity began to reveal itself, the subtle impression of something beneath the surface of my uncertain self, underneath my mind's melancholic fits. A spirit-entity.

It needed no fear or self-doubt, and had none. While the cities filled me with dread, the wilds began to transform me with peace and stillness. As a result, the being in me was growing, like an ephemeral face that appeared at times from behind a gauzy veil. I was becoming more and more aware of it, conscious of the thing in me, awakening to the nearness of the metaphysical recesses inside me, and my inhibition and discouragement were subsequently relaxed.

When I lay about in fields and watched the full moon, a hush would descend on the spot. The being in me would glide away in the moonlight, upward to dizzy heights, across the fields, lingering to look at the stars until the dawn came. All a fantasy, but I let go and floated in the universe. After midnight, reality tended to become distorted. In the darkness and remoteness, my interior came alive to walk the world without the slightest hesitation.

14

I found the sensation of vastness in a tiny leaf. By looking at it, things exploded with mystery, became a great limitlessness. The mystical has a tendency to eliminate the surface, and in its presence my surface self became a hallucination. The I in me was replaced more and more by the drifting being further within. Nothing was real. Moreover, nothing needed to be real. It was perfectly natural for me to lie down languidly with amplified emotions but not a single moving limb, not a bit of concern, only a liberation brought on by reveling in the mysterious. The majestic starlight overhead encouraged me to abandon myself, and I desired nothing out there, needed nothing, was nothing of my former self. I felt the universal excite my senses, my oblivious mind, my heightened feelings. My objective became only to lose restraint. And out there, I returned to health. I became an inconspicuous and feverish dream while some magic was worked that quickened my mind until I was aware, awakened, filled with a primal essence. My anxieties dropped away in the night. Magic became the heart of existence, and the emotional knowledge I gained by being in plain sight of it became the whole of my education.

I developed a sense that within me was something of value. It was something universal and beyond reproach. It was quite an optimistic feeling after my earlier years. Outwardly, I may have looked haggard and worn. I wore the same dirty clothes every day. I stopped shaving. I let my hair go unkempt. My wanderings over the mountains often left me sickly-looking, pale, and too exhausted for ordinary conversation. Up all night, by morning I was removed entirely from the ordinary and thus found it difficult to appear ordinary. But inwardly I dressed myself in the exquisite robes of my underlying nature. It linked me to everything. Like skin touching the air, the skin of my interior pressed against the spiritual. It became habitual to look upon things as one whole. My own essential being belonged to the intertwined, the incorporeal undercurrent that was the essence of everything. I stood alongside the hidden realms and dissolved into them, and though my exterior crumbled, though it even looked menacing from time to time, my interior, my being, was loosening.

15

I became more and more disposed toward flights of fantasy. I wandered for hours in a hazy and indefinite dream, through groves of trees and thick meadowland. I was educated by the unpopulated realms, by the gentler art of studying flowers, by pondering existence where the sense of existence was magnified, and I learned thereby the value of beauty: it brought me into contact with something more innately human and good than all I'd previously experienced. To a great extent, I'd adapted to my situation, and in doing so, I'd inadvertently begun to escape the circumstances that had made me lose heart to begin with. The melancholic feeling of being unaccepted by society served at length to propel me toward places where I felt less disheartened, less spiritless, less oppressed by the stagnant hardness of ordinary life. Discouragement with life left me in poor spirits, but when the night came on, my tender moods followed. My wholehearted desire to find something more than that hardened world, that inevitably hostile world in which I'd grown up, pushed me until I found myself at a soothing, ephemeral distance away from it.

It was a calmer place, and I moved toward it beneath the moonlight, the rainfall, and the skies both clouded and starry. I lived a pastoral existence, enjoying myself in solitude, lonesome but elated when the storms would come at night, when the rainclouds would cover the sky in great billows of gray, when the rain would drop over the mountains, sweeping down in sheets of purple that bled into the purple of the distance. The meadows were infinite, with countless vistas overlooking countless expansive landscapes like paintings made of nature. The landscapes had a way of evoking journeys, setting out toward distant places, through magnificent trees, obscured paths, dirt roads that led deep into the wilds of the withdrawn and faraway.

They inspired me to search for something more.

One night, I'd gone out to wander all night in idleness, to luxuriate in the meadows. I'd lain back in the grass. Above me a white moon was looking down, having emerged from behind black rainclouds, like a draped white sheet. It had a ghostly countenance and seemed all the more glorified just then. I clasped my hands over my chest and watched for half an hour, under the influence of strange sensations. The rainclouds swirled over my head like a magical spectacle, with the moon glowing through them and elsewhere a congealed darkness to them as black as smoke. In the woods, there were owls crooning. Strange creatures clawed onto branches, dark shapes that cried then flitted away. I could hardly move.

Everything struck me at once. The feeling of tenderness came into me; the rain that night, just a sprinkling of it, seemed itself to be gentler; the moon was somehow more benevolent and warm. Looking across the mountains beside me, the distance was dark, the furthest distance looking like the rainclouds were sweeping down from a thousand miles overhead. Everything in the moment was made soft and transcendent. It soothed me with its beauty and alleviated my cares. I felt nearly amorous in the dark, as if rapport with the massive scope of things were possible just by being amidst its massiveness.

A moment later, I stood and walked on in a trance-like state, a kind of clouded mirth mingled with a clarity of perception, gazing around me into a world differing from the ordinary one. I was in bliss. Sight was harder, but my emotions were intensified, with the inexplicable in everything just then. I saw beneath the surface, deep down into the depths, the underground, the hidden insides. My face was transfixed. My awareness was sharp. My body merged with the night. My eyes looked about, a dreaming pair of eyes, and I saw wondrous images: shadows like other-worldly creatures, black trees pressed against the sky like watchers. My sensations were the fantastical in my consciousness. The rain came down dizzily from above, a swirl in the light wind. I looked up into it, beneath the entirety of the sky, and watched the white haze around the moon as it passed through an empty space in the clouds.

It was all perhaps a figment of my imagination, perhaps an illusion, but I had the feeling that the whole experience was the incubation of something. Everywhere in my vision, permeating me, were a myriad of magnificent things, moment by moment flooding my senses like infinitely entangled space. It was an unbelievable fantasy that I dared not disbelieve to view myself conjoining with something out there in the dark. Because in my otherwise solitary life, I had a great deal of need for it.

16

I was different. I was a ghost in an old photograph. I was a pale image escaping from life. I often wondered about things that others might have found unappealing. My thoughts were equally spent in contemplation of the beautiful and the morbid. It seemed to me that something was to be learned as much from the hideous as from the sublime. I longed for something more from life, whether it was gained from a jaunt through the early-morning woods to watch the sunrise or from a night spent wandering the dark landscapes in order to feel something more mysterious than the mundanity of the ordinary, which was frightening to me. I went out and everything would begin, reality would disappear, and the undercurrent of life would rise up from the depths. It would change all outward appearances, giving them an emotional character, something felt intuitively, largely impossible to witness in a crowded street but entangling me in wistfulness and the invisible, a world beneath appearances, beneath superficial consciousness.

Most of the night, I lingered out of sight in solitude. I knew a secret existence. I'd awaken like a nightmare, my hair in tousled disarray. I'd crawl from bed like a night creature and go mesmerized into the mountains, into a cold, ghostly world. I wanted freedom from restraint, and my method was to lose myself. The night had a pulse, filled with sights, a vaguely sensuous moon, black shadows cast into the black distance, tree limbs moving in the eerie wind, and the spectacle of stars overhead, all of which seemed to be giving me direction. I contented myself by letting go, and I found that the root of my being awaited me to do so.

Without companionship, I was inclined toward a vagueness of being. I lingered in an isolated mental landscape, the world replaced by the solace of reveries and the essence of dreams. I made a renunciation of sorts. I loved the world most when night fell and life seemed to slip away. Night was a lucid dream, and because I was discovering the surreal under its surface, I decided to remain awake in its presence. I found in it something gauzy to my senses, meaningful in the way a dream might suggest to a conflicted person what should be done, and I became inseparable from it.

Night after night, I performed my escape, explored, ambled through the late-night woods, living a secret life. I went out to vanish in the dark. The entirety of the ordinary world was removed for a time, having fallen away while the strange and impossible became the truth in front of me. I felt an uncanny awareness in the dark, as if the impossible were inside everything, and a strange attraction to that underlying impossibility propelled me forward. The nights became many nights, nights that went on endlessly, stranger than anything I'd known. They suggested something inexpressible, as if the weird were closer to the truth of things, and the inexpressible became my guide.

One night, I meandered through the hazy air till dawn. The horizon began to glow red. Even the trees had a ruddy sheen to their branches and trunks. I looked across the landscape: The ordinary had ceased to exist. The mist had begun to clear, now hovering in the still air like a thin film of light. The wildflowers and the leaves of bushes, still glistening wet, started to shine with the sunrise. And I felt entirely unrestricted by fear. My being flourished with a strange euphoria. It was an awakening. My eyes were just then flickering open. I felt a fleeting impression beneath everything I saw. It was like a dream or a recollection, a distance in the eyes that had existed for millions of years which belonged to the very heart of being.

17

In large part, I began life averse to life. I felt little kinship with people until later, after more spiritual experiences changed me. Until my mind changed, I simply disliked being alive on the planet. I began to transform after I spent time alone, when I developed a love for what was interior.

The first experience I'd had in childhood. The second came on in the same fashion, while I walked the mountains as a young man, as I walked alone along a strange dirt road. I'd been depressed that night, but the longer I roamed and the deeper my legs pushed me into the uninhabited, the more I felt set free.

I was shortly in the middle of nowhere, following wonders, my imagination coming alive. The wind blowing over the tops of the mountains was miraculous. Cold, but filled with a power beyond reason. The grass blew and my raincoat blew around me, but I felt no chill, no shivering. As time passed, an elaborate timelessness began to take shape in the dark. It was the ephemeral and the universal. At such times, the underlying causes of life seem to long for recognition. The grayish-looking trees stood up from their patches of dirt and caught my eye. I stopped to look at one of them.

I stood in that annihilating darkness for twenty minutes. I hardly blinked. My eyesight sharpened and I was mesmerized by the tree as if it were the gateway to a temple. It was hardly a collection of bark and leaves. Instead, it seemed to stretch backward in time. Once a sapling, before that a seed. And before that: Where did it all come from? Everything in time had gone into this one tree. It had a family, predecessors, and those themselves stretched back to the first cells on the planet, the first of everything. It had begun with the dust of some supernova. It had been part of the first atoms ever to have existed. It was the beginning of the universe. At one point in time, every infinitesimal particle in the tree had belonged to a timeless singularity. One timeless dot. And there it was, the whole universe, after billions of years, embodied by the tree standing before me.

Nothing but reverence filled me. I relaxed and let go, lost all concern, felt my depression lift, and my being unraveled in the dark. I eyed the landscape ahead and continued along the path, which wound upwards into the night, through trees, over meadows. The entire world was dependent on everything in it. It was a whole. Within it was a timeless intricacy, an interwoven essence that contained all things. Nothing else needed to make sense.

18

To unloosen the love in the being it's sometimes only necessary to look hard at something alive. To stare at a tree for twenty minutes awakens a certain sense of the universe. As I walked along, I felt my limbs disappear, my body float. I walked with an amazing comfort, the annihilation of myself under the dizzy stars, a madness and a delight. To discover the universal in something alive was my second of such experiences, and such experiences scarcely ceased thereafter. They're remarkable for the elation they provide. The equivalent might be to make love. To take delight in a body that houses a living being is a miraculous experience. It intensifies the feeling of being alive, that strange mystery of being, until starry-eyed and dazzled, everything is holy: a naked body, the face of a lover, the fingers examining skin.

Just as the bodies of lovers feel themselves conjoined when making love, the being of a person joins together with all life in the midst of the wilds. I lost myself like a lover into the obliteration that comes when contemplating vastness. I saw a tree as the embodiment of every tree that came before it, its entire history an inheritance that came even from ancient stars. And there was a oneness just then to the whole of existence. A powerful sense that beyond the limits a unification was the definition of things. It entranced me. And I was in love, like a mystic in love with the earth and the universe.

19

At first, I'd questioned the universe, and soon after, I'd blamed the universe. I'd criticized the world, I'd made my morbid critique of human existence, which I'd then thrown into the garbage. But I made my escape. My escape was the mountains, the hillsides stretching endlessly, nobody around. I lost myself while wandering through places that had all the makings of another, different world. Many nights, I stood gazing from the cliffs, because something called me to the edge. The wind would sweep through the trees and the clouded sky would move to reveal a bright moon. I was up there like a ghost, night after night, haunting the borderland between life and death.

I ran away, left the world, went into the night. I found myself far from human life, and I vanished. The trees whipped, and the wind was fierce like the end of it all, blowing my raincoat out. Nothing could be seen but green hills, black trees, and clouds coming from the distance and passing into the distance again, back to the ordinary world. I felt the vastness flood my bloodstream. The sight of an ant on a twig was miraculous. It was a very small part of something great and graceful, soft and holy.

Suddenly the entire universe enters the mind through the dark spots of the pupils. It's large enough to rip the seams of the skull, filling the mind to bursting with thoughts of tenderness, decorating the innermost recesses with the sensuality of midnight and starlight and an inviolate lifelong love: inexhaustible, unchangeable. A new perception is made possible. Nothing is the same as it was before.

Out there in the wilds, the universe seemed to look down upon me. Beneath the sky, I felt the world differently. It was a single organism. I was part of something vast, the sky and the woods, the people and the insects. Everything on earth was one body. It had a healthy complexion, a vigorous nature, and it filled me with a profoundly meaningful array of sensations. I had only to sit underneath the stars to find a sense of awe that would last for days.

I'd shiver in the cold, but I was learning. My social paralysis was being peeled off layer by layer. My psychological torments were being given healing medicine. I'd shudder beneath the mystery of the night sky, but I'd return home with a benevolence inside me for the whole of the earth, its beauty and its charm, its griefs and its guilts. When I saw the pain in the face of a stranger, when I saw someone afraid of ridicule, when I saw someone afraid of everything, I felt empathy well up within me and come out like unblocked love in electrified doses. After the world became, as a whole, an old, slow, long-lived being, my feelings toward everything on it were tender ever after.

20

I went outside, as I did every night, prepared to spend the night exploring, because I ached for something more. I went beyond the little black gate at the foot of the mountains. It opened to the forbidding path of gravel that went off into darkness; nondescript, but entering the eerie. I started the climb, traveling along, the crunch of rocks beneath my boots letting me know I was leaving the civilized neighborhoods. I passed the run-down farmhouse with its little lit-up window. Above me the night was full of stars, a swarm of stars that blazed, shimmered, glistened, and hovered like tiny blurred droplets of white. There were a few stands of trees at first, then more. As I got higher up, I came to the mountain meadows. I wandered into them, a haze of gray mist hanging over the grass, and the grass went on endlessly.

Having climbed for a few miles, I opened the unbarred gate of the old cemetery. I had to pass through it. I examined the decayed headstones as I walked. They were toppled over, broken, with a black mossy substance coating them. Far from the city, far from modern civilization, a particular grave, the grave of an old woman, still stood high. She had once been a dabbler in medicine who was said to have been a witch. She had died in a high-speed stagecoach crash on her way to help a sick person in a nearby village. Her burial had been strange. A storm had come when they'd tried to bury her, making it impossible. They had needed to wait several days before attempting it again. After she had finally been buried, her ghost had been seen, here and there at first. The sightings continued for two hundred years. She was said to haunt the region at night, giving those mountains the first story of their reputation for being haunted.

I passed through the old cemetery and continued upward into the meadows that lay still in the dark. I lingered here and there, beside dark trees, at the apex of mountains, looking up into the sky, watching the moon, marveling at the sights. The openness of the landscape was always delightful, its miles and miles of undulating hillsides, its dark emptiness like a wild world from another realm of existence. Out there, surrounded by unbound nature lying beneath the universe, I felt rejuvenated. Life thrived around me, and the feeling I had was powerful enough to transform me with tranquility. It was in that haunted landscape that I first came alive. In those days, I could be found wandering idly, here and there, like a young ghost who could be seen doing nothing in particular, like a ghost does, a wandering spirit seen in the dark going up and down the mountainsides. Nevertheless, I was discovering the vastness of another world, landscapes I could explore to be at peace, and in doing so, I inadvertently discovered the interior of things. I encountered out there the unfathomable essence, an immaterial underlying nature, a deeper character beneath the elaborate hallucination of reality, and the effect was permanent.

21

These days, I'm pulled toward the inside of myself. Deep down in the dark, I find a gleaming diamond. It's the luminous, glittering stone of introverted essence, and the beauty of it is where everything begins. When I feel near to it, when I feel it in a living thing, I wonder what it's like to die, because the sensation of something so grandiose as living becomes magnified.

In moments of clarity, I know the same secret lies within everyone, underneath the material world. I can imagine that late at night, when anyone is alone, lying in bed, staring upward in the dark, aware, seeing with truer eyes, something remarkable blooms inside, fed by the being.

I'm dissatisfied with life in general, and the prison of life is in every cell of my body, as it is with anyone. I'm free as far as a human being is capable, but after all, a dog will urinate on another dog's urine without much comprehension of why, and its ability to stop itself is limited by its natural instincts.

Nevertheless, in spite of all this, what hides in the heart of a person is sanctified, and when I'm there in its presence, awake to it, clarified in my vision, I think the melancholy thought that when it dies something will have been lost that should be exempt from dying.

What lingers is not a doubt about the worthiness of life, but a certainty that something remarkable is happening on earth. Whatever the case may be, a person is not in possession of the intangible facet of life that's been welling up from within for millennia. The crux of being is sanctified. It inspires visions of poetry, love of revelation. It's felt when seeing the sunrise or the sunset, when the observer watches as the moon peaks up on the horizon and begins to ascend the night sky, when the stars themselves begin to sway on a night when all the universe seems drunk with wine.

The being in everyone is majestic. Therefore, if life demands coldness and indecency in order for a living thing to survive, if it demands a certain hardness of heart, then it's all the more magnificent when the living thing decides rather to rebel against the nature of living and submit instead to the only true beauty: an abstract, entranced, altogether unconstrained devotion to love.

22

I was more than dissatisfied throughout my childhood. By the time I entered adolescence, I was already growing sick, feeling imprisoned in a lackluster world. Because I'd projected my homelife onto the whole of the world, that world seemed filled with materialism and hostility. And that at the expense of human potential. I steered away from it. I lay in bed at night dreaming of the Renaissance. All day, I studied books on painting, read about the lives of artists and thinkers, and made my own efforts to create things, because I longed for something different. Instead of the world in which I found myself, I wanted to live in an exciting world that created something magnificent enough to honor human nature.

All the while, I was becoming more and more rebellious. And morbid. I had a terrible suspicion toward life, under the influence as I was of a vaguely misanthropic revulsion. I longed to distance myself from everything, all the shallow and drab occupations, the materialistic monotony, the wasted lives for the sake of luxury. At least, that was part of the reason I left. Partly, it was a distaste for the way things were that made me leave; partly, however, it was an unbearable fear of the way things were.

For years, my life was one of aversion. I dropped out of high school, too depressed, and from then on my education was self-directed. I went out every night to wander. I often wandered the streets, which could be quite dangerous at night, but I hardly worried about being mugged or murdered because my life didn't matter much to me.

I sat beneath trees in parks without people. I took long walks for a dozen miles up into the mountains. I studied the violet colors of the sunset and the purple colors of twilight. Then struck out through groves of trees, lay down in the dirt and watched the stars, found the romantic moon. I lived a life completely free of the constraints of society, educated enough by the poetry of landscapes and the timeless feeling that came over me late at night when I stood alone in some of the most entrancing environments possible.

Of all the reasons I left, it was my father who had the largest influence. His violence was such that it turned me on to gentler modes of living. I lay in bed one night and determined to be soft. I wanted a high-minded peace. I wholeheartedly wished to avoid any lifestyle that would lead me into the company of men like him. Thus, he was the model of my antithesis. That type of antagonistic influence has an enormous effect on a life thereafter.

The opposite? It was a life among flowers. It was to consider the nature of existence in the midst of a dark forest landscape, to climb high up into the mountains, all alone, and look out upon the world everywhere below with a breathless awe. For me, these were all about gentleness. The fields on some far-distant mountain filled me with a sense of civility and love and beauty, a sense of the divine vein that ran through the whole of life.

However, that divine vein went against nothing. As far as it was concerned, nothing was lackluster. Materialism wasn't condemned as it was by me, nor was anything else. Instead, whatever existed was accepted, everything and everyone as they were, without criticism, without any desire to eye others with suspicion. Moreover, without any ability to do so. And unbeknownst to me, my experiences therefore contained a panacea, a complete remedy for all my troubles.

In short, for the sake of ease, I began to employ my sense of being to find comfort around others. I found by doing so that, more and more, because my being made no judgments or criticisms, the vaguely misanthropic tendencies that had been developing in me simply fell away. I'd probably begun to dislike all the things I disliked because, in some form, I felt a sense of rejection surrounding them. However, when I concentrated my attention, I could feel no antagonism coming from within people, internally, at the core, even if externally I was met with it quite often.

When in that place, the core, I saw no distinction between my individual essence and the essence in others. Everything was the same, the same essence, a divine interior that had roots in something ancient, something incredible buried deep beneath the surface. It was like a great universal field. Only the exterior changed, lived out individual lives, had idiosyncratic traits expressed by individuals. Interiorly, every being shared the same qualities. Because I loved the being in me without fear, I loved the being in every person without fear, as theirs and mine were the same elemental essence, the subterranean watcher, the non-critic, the innermost eyes that gazed out lovingly.

Everything began to solidify. I saw that an internal universality existed inside me, conjoined with the same universality in everything else. It brought me into contact with something inextricably linked, a deeper, more placid character within everyone. While I remained anxious in the cities, hesitant out of habit, I began to long for people just the same, and I was less and less fearful when they were near. Soon enough I was entering into bliss when in a crowd rather than feeling the need to withdraw. The whole thing was pleasurable, like love. I found myself enamored of everyone around me, at a bus stop, in the grocery store, amidst the crowds in the streets. I was soothed by the being in others.

The quest I'd endeavored to take, to go out into the wilds of the world in order to be alone, was due to my irreconcilable oddness and fear. The very things that led me away brought me into contact with the essential nature of life. I came to know the inmost being in all things. I was more and more ecstatic, entering inside, looking from this place inside. From there, I directed my attention to the inner landscape of others, and without fail their magnificence disclosed itself to me. The result was the blooming of an intimate essence, a divine vein, a gracefulness inside everything around me, and then love.

23

Mt. Diablo – the Devil's mountain. I'd go out in the rain, in the cold, and walk into the nowhere of the world in order to learn something of life from the landscapes, from the moonlight, from being wet with rain under the night sky, under the suspicion even then that the morning dew spread thickly over a field of flowers would enlighten my senses and awaken my mind. I perambulated the dark. I stood atop the hillsides gazing down into the darkness everywhere below. I searched for a trace of something, looking at all the stars, and I hoped. I was up there for a year, like some wild thing, searching the mountains for a sign of it.

Once that beauty is first seen, the stark contrast of the world in comparison is painful to see: heartbreak, broken dreams, unfairness, injustice, prejudice, the rich and the poor, the healthy and the sick, countries everywhere in constant conflict. All these years later, I understand that that beauty was my education. It taught me to find the truer nature of everything, to look beneath the veil, to look within human beings, delving down until I found the essence in them, beneath the undoubtedly strange world of being alive.

24

The moon rises slowly over the forest. It floods everything with a pale light. In the distance, the mountains are languid and luxuriating, and the trees are as black as the sky. I'm overcome by the sense of something so vast that I feel outside time and space. I exist in the ephemeral, the inexpressible. I stood by the window looking out into the night, up to the moon and into the mountains and the trees, and I saw. No more real than anything in my imagination, a reflection of another, deeper world – the invisible, or perhaps a dream. Sometimes a person becomes something else: the moonlight, the night sky, the way the wind comes through the trees. Sometimes a person leaves the world altogether and becomes the magical, the mystical, something far stranger than what's perceivable on earth.

25

My mother owned a cabin in the woods. I went out there. I'd have the whole place to myself, and the solitude appealed to me quite a bit. I hadn't seen the place since my mother divorced my father.

I took a bus there. As the passengers loaded on, I seated myself at the back of the bus in order to be somewhat hidden. Backpacks were stuffed into the overhead compartments. Some people settled into their seats and put in headphones, some slumped into naps, some began chattering back and forth with the other passengers. When the bus departed, the sun had already set and the sky outside grew dark quickly. A man I'd seen sipping from a flask went into the bathroom to vomit. He seemed to whimper.

As the bus drove through the night, I was in a happy frame of mind. I'd left everything behind and it seemed as if serenity would come at last. Throughout the night, I was awake. The bus made stops. One or two passengers emptied off. Everyone else was asleep. In the dark, I looked around at the passengers. Outside were panoramic views of long, flat farmland under the moonlight, which filled me with reverence. And inside were sleeping people I found myself adoring with the same reverence. Unique beings. Beautiful lives. I sat in the dark, hidden, and felt an exquisite tenderness for them just then. I relaxed and let go. I was the only one awake, and it was the first chance I'd had in a long while, there in the dark, to take a long look at people. Like falling in love, I moved closer to the inmost in them, imagined enfolding them in my arms, looked upon them with soft eyes, burst into bloom.

When I reached the cabin, it was the same old rickety and rustic place. The windows looked out upon towering trees and countless stars. The moon was in the sky, lighting up the forest. Grayish trees stood outside in the moonlight like sentinels guarding the night. When I stepped onto the deck, their smell was the rough smell of sap and pine needles.

Altogether, the place was perfect. A great forest stretched everywhere around it. Thousands of trees could be seen climbing up the distant mountainsides. The sky was clearer than any I'd seen. Nobody lived nearby. The world was vacant for miles around. I found myself in a glorious woodland paradise, and I sat on the deck for an hour exulting in the bright moon in the black sky, which was to become a great friend over the next year.

26

When I look back on my childhood, I understand who I was in a way that I couldn't have then. I was one of the invisible of the world, those children whose lives are nearly dead after too much hopelessness has got hold of them. The continual erosion from a bad homelife wears them down until little is left. Schoolteachers might wonder why they look sad and uncomfortable, but nothing can be done unless they have broken bones and black eyes. There aren't any laws against screaming at them all day.

By ten years old, I'd been thoroughly indoctrinated into a sense of inferiority by my father. Even at ten years old, I was in constant anxiety, feeling second-rate, with a wavering voice and an ingrained feeling of insignificance. As a result, I looked upon the world as a place for others, while for my part, by the end of the first decade of my life, I was so inhibited I could hardly speak. Making a phone call was hard. Talking to a waiter to order a meal with my family at a restaurant frightened me. Being in a crowded street made me suffocate.

I fumbled over everything, mired in self-criticism on my way through the world, falling down, feeling frightened the instant I saw a group of my peers enjoying themselves. I feared being unlikable so I never expected to be liked. I grieved, dispirited and heartsick, until the suffering was stamped with bitterness into my memories. It seemed there was no way out, no acceptance to be had by society, and worse, no reason for any of it. It was the worst kind of suffering: meaningless suffering. Because it was so meaningless, I looked for a means to give it meaning. To justify my pains, I cultivated a great deal of empathy for others. I made the decision to be soft, with consciousness of their suffering and a disposition mindful of causing as little harm as possible.

27

Life on earth isn't adapted to perfection. That is, it's still evolving in the mud, like a mud worm lives, learning to survive its life. Every living thing has a dirty face.

Thus, I allow myself candor. I allow for everything: any thought, any emotion, any desire. It's essential. Honesty helps in learning what lies buried deep in the mind. I can't be free unless I admit the shadow self and examine it without self-censorship. I often find ugly things. To know myself, the underlying causes of my personality, it's necessary to look at the ugly thoughts, emotions, and desires. They may be thoroughly unwanted, but they'll never disclose their presence and will continue to hold influence as long as self-censorship is in place.

Instead, I cultivate a longing to see. I allow myself to become disturbed. Even sickened. In order to do this I remember that I am not I. The world flows about, in part as me, as if I were the culmination of a billion moments. But I'm neither the world nor the self the world has made. The elaborate hallucination isn't the whole of things. I'm a being beneath it, full of empathy, as if enlisted to empathize. It's ready to look, allowing the ugly, the distasteful, even the hellish. At the inmost, there's no identity and thus no identifying with any of it, none of the ugliness or shadowy complexities. Thus nothing is scary, nothing is hidden, and nothing escapes my desire to see.

Likewise, I don't care to take offense to anything a person says or does. A person is neither the world nor the self the world has made. Another person's actions might come from a private torment, from unseen agonies, from pains I might not understand, but an unmistakable being exists beneath the hallucination. It shares the same existence as my own. While the surface has been troubled, has gone through much unknown hardship that might ensure an acidic, disturbing personality in anyone, the interior below it is what I want to see.

On a bus, a man in his thirties sat in front of me sipping from a flask. He was thoroughly drunk, hair in disarray, face oily, talking to his friends beside him, sharing his flask. I was on my way to the library, doing a study of one of the world wars or some such thing, and we both got off at the same stop. He staggered off the bus behind me, slumped shoulders, a hint of a vengeful expression in his face as he looked around at the street. As he was putting his flask in his coat pocket, I asked him what time it was. He was shocked. Clearly taken aback, seriously offended, he half-screamed at me, angrily: "I don't have a watch!"

His reaction was startling to me. But I discovered I took no offense to it. Instead of stopping at the surface, I paused and imagined the inmost in him, beneath the mundane world and all its difficulties, beneath the hostility with which he'd blurted out an answer to my question. I could feel my eyes soften instantly. In there was the thing that made us both alike, removed us and everyone else from the exterior that was so full of suffering. The need for anything else, any offense taken, any scowl or scorn-fulness as a response, was erased by empathy, a comprehension that everyone has their own woes, that struggles often end in defeated mentalities, and a sensation of peace came over me.

These days when I deal with people, I see their elemental qualities are the same as mine, and I let the complexities of the surface fall away. Perhaps the man on the bus had wounds that ran deep and caused bitter hostility, but when I moved closer to his interior, the unconditioned being was there, visible to my imagination, with nothing of hostility in it. I see it in people, a lovable innermost aspect. Its presence has the tendency to inspire joy, like a newborn, a life before any experiences have compli-cated it with bad memories and bitterness.

If I stop and stand in a crowd in this mood, I lose myself, feeling the same reverence for the people in it as I would for the most magnificent natural landscapes, the Grand Canyon or the mountains of Yosemite. People are breathtakingly mysterious. They're sometimes full of agonies and griefs, even wretchedness at times, but they're also undoubtedly powerful embodiments of something incomprehensibly vast, impossible lives, living things with no known cause or even reason for being, personifications of the whole of something larger, more magical than imaginable. I look on lovingly, with no need for judgment or criticism, no anger when mistreated, no possibility of taking offense, until I'm suitably drunk on the feeling I get from it.

28

Extraordinary feelings come when alone in the presence of the majestic, alone in the sense of being secure in one's self. If a person is secure when within, a hillside of flowers might reveal hidden universes filled with deities. A cliffside might be overlooking the greatest hope ever known. Feelings might rise that melt the whole ego down to nothing, so that the love within bursts forth unabated for hours, like constant bliss.

Pleasant sensations are easier to experience when alone, because people have a tendency to come back up to the surface when in the presence of others. It's due to fear. Fear cancels the deeper self, especially the love it has within it. A raving lunatic is often not a nice person. If you see one on the street, the raving lunatic might be cursing everyone around in a whisper. The fear is too great. The painfulness of it is too extreme. What's done is to transform that fear into hatred, which is so often the case with fear. Fear becomes all sorts of rationalized hostilities: rudeness, aggressiveness, a spiteful attitude. At the core, it's just fear. A raving lunatic is often senseless with fear. It's too bad. It's a sad thing. It's no good for the person, and the suffering is painful. It's an example, however, of how fear closes off the deeper self and the love it has.

29

Private landscapes of the mind are where love is first found. It extends from there. A mind adrift in incoherent senselessness will find congenial feelings rarely expressed in the domain of human beings, except when in love. And it's the object to be consumed by these feelings. In the daylight hours to take what's found in the twilight hours of love and distribute it, to experience the mind unbound and lose civilized standards until the dreamy landscapes remove all impairments, and then to give that love away to anyone who wants it.

Because true love is unconditional. Not given according to rank. But given without thought. It has no values, no standards, no judgments, no biases. Instead, it verges on a bliss that can't be contained. It's a beautiful thing. And in any case, the complications of life go nowhere, result in nothing but more complications. At the root of conflict is competition, building it up, leading to further complications. At the root of unhappiness is judgment, standards and the rest, creating a conditional mentality without freedom. But to give love freely is to give it unconditionally, without thought for competing interests. The magnitude of feeling that results is that of a universe entering the mind through the pupils.

30

These days it feels as if all my life were a celebration of my unhinged mind. To live is to be on the verge of the sublime. Bliss is just beneath the surface. It waits in my being, a simultaneously elevated and obliterated state of mind. When under the influence of bliss, of the bliss in the being, a trance is induced and everything is holy. The dirt. The flowers. The trees. People are part of the interconnection of everything. Part of the dirt, the flowers, the trees. Every part of life is part of everything in life. Every cell is part of a greater, boundless body. Existence is an ever-present moment, a lucid joy, an immeasurable behemoth, a merging of all things with no division. The universe is a whole, together, an interrelated macrocosm with nothing excluded from its interdependence. The ever-present moment is connected with every previous moment, and everything contains a trace of the beginning. When under the influence of bliss, of the bliss found inside, of the being's perpetually elated nature, the world becomes strange and different. It educates with poetry. The stars become a magical spectacle of the far-distant, the way infinity seems expressed in the tiny points of light. All life becomes miraculous, a unified totality, an endlessly interwoven fabric. Everything is in harmony, like the music of the spheres.

31

The being in me might as well be love, since love is the only thing I feel when I go for a visit. It's an abstract mood. Ecstatic but calm. Euphoric. Neither liking nor disliking anything, the being watches without attachment, fascinated enough to watch for the length of a life. It sees cruelty, embarrassment, rage, anguish, bitterness, fear. And it does so with the utmost compassion, because the essence of the being is unconditional love. It remains untouched, untarnished, unharmed by anything in life, like an untroubled ecstasy that forever replenishes itself. While I go about my life, I can feel the observer inside me enchanted with observation, enthusiastic about experience. And during the roughest times, I can return inward for escape, as I've done quite often. When peace and contentedness are needed, the being is welcoming, a pure awareness, like clarity in the aftermath of a truth, offering the openhearted smile unique to unconditional love.

32

When the expression comes up that we're all alone, that we're essentially alone, live alone and die alone, I feel awkward as if approaching the absurd. I don't feel alone in that sense. I've been lonely, distant from life and people, discreet with my heart, disconnected from what others are doing with their lives. But when ecstatic, it becomes clear. At the core of people, everyone is the same, with the same needs. Most people want similar things at heart. Desires are shared desires. Disappointments have a similar pattern. People may go about acquiring what they want differently. Sure, I can't see into the mind of someone else. But I can see into their humanity simply by being human.

These days, it's easy for me to become enraptured with the soul of another person. It's easy for me to feel bliss when surrounded by living beings. Sometimes I slow down, my hands become gentle, and I feel the ecstasy of being with others. Euphoria. Fearlessness. Love. The most corrupted and vile person has depths beyond understanding. This is supremely important to understand. These depths can be felt, and when felt are never specific to that one person. They're specific to the whole. They're the idiosyncrasies of an adorable, timeless newborn that has no aversion and is a delight to love. When am I alone when I have the whole of life within me?

We aren't essentially alone, but instead are essentially the same vital force of amazement and amiability. We're the imaginative being of unsophisticated naturalness whose heredity is sensitive and gemlike in its facets. Multifaceted. When dejected, which is so often the case, the fragile person grimaces and snuffs it out, becomes forgetful of it, tries to keep up good manners but remains stiff, oppressed by fear, lingers about in that limbo where uncertainties, inferiority complexes, and egomania perpetually pit one against the other. But being alone is more like an opinion, a view, a perspective. Remove all viewpoints and the pure self touches the distinct feature of life that threads through everything without exception.

33

The observer is closest to the truth. Beneath the surface, the being is the witness in the mind that steps aside in self-examination, observes the conditioned mind reacting. The being is the watcher. The religion of the being is to love. From inside, the being in me delights to look outside, feeling the pleasant sensation of a warm, candid empathy toward individuals. Even when I make mistakes, even when my flaws are seen, they aren't bothersome to it. With a benevolent disposition, it wants only to gaze lovingly at my life and to watch the tales of my life play out, one after the other, happy or sad. If I do questionable things, it remains comfortable and adoring. Throughout my life, it follows the themes of my life, my idiosyncrasies, my strengths and faults, as if that were the purpose of its existing. Without dissatisfaction, unpretentious and nonjudgmental, it simply observes, the watcher, the witness, alert for when it's needed, and when needed, it unfurls, filled with peace, overwhelming even an uncomfortable wretch like me with its love, acceptance, compassion, empathy, and the charming way it comforts with elation.

34

While I sat nervously in a train station, on my way about the world, surrounded by all manner of shy passengers, I saw a familiar situation play out. I watched as an angry, disgruntled woman passing through the station spoke up with hatred for everyone around her. She was full of rage, nearly tearing at others with her speech. She was practicing what's practiced when fear is unbearable and overwhelming and hatred is a step upward from anxiety.

I watched her, aware of her fear, aware of its resemblance to my fear. Others acted with good manners, allowing the madwoman to lay bitterness on them, and I dropped off into a mood. The affairs of people, with their seemingly endless ability to frustrate at times, are so often filled with a communicable distress, like a noiseless alarm continually ringing inside every brain.

The angry woman was captive, imprisoned in a private mentality. Likely, someone or something had hurt her. An entire lifetime may have hurt her. Life has the tendency to hurt everyone. And as is usually the case, the hatred in her speech was a disguise, an attempt to counterbalance frightened feelings with a demeaning response, to compensate for feelings of inferiority with feelings of superiority. And she had disposed of restraint by this point.

Nobody knows the inner workings of strangers enough to hate them. However, in a fit of terror born by being in proximity to a frightening crowd, hatred and criticism and judgment, even mental faultfinding and mental belittling, directed toward others effectively counteract the horrified nerves. They succeed in alleviating the fear that circles about in the mind, the fear that makes the brain feel as if it were swimming in it. I watched as she cursed everyone under her breath, making her way through the crowd as if to oppose anyone in her way.

35

Like the madwoman in the train station, everyone builds a system of coping mechanisms to help them deal with life. Disassembling those coping mechanisms, which are conditioned, is a way out, a path to freedom. And because the mind will form them naturally, everyone has them to some degree. They are deeply ingrained in the psyche, and involve some of the most intricate complexes that make up the identity.

Thus when dissolved, something remarkable happens. When I realized the extent to which I'd been living my life opposed to my father, a great number of my views changed. I hadn't expected it. I'd associated hostility with quite a bit of things that really had nothing of it in them. I became mute for hours and wrote out a list of things I'd taken an antagonistic position toward because they reminded me of my unhappy childhood. Not surprisingly, most of my views with regard to those things simply fell away.

They were self-protective views. I'd held things in contempt because I'd learned they led to ill manners. I'd associated materialism, for instance, with my father's outbursts. Materialism itself had seemed to help in disrupting the natural flow of my peaceful existence. I'd connected it with ignorance, blame, faultfinding, the irritant of being a psychological ruin – and being satisfied with that.

Yet, when I looked on it freshly, it wasn't the source of despicable behavior. Without the need to defend myself, I relaxed my position. A materialistic brute wasn't threatening me anymore and so my adamant stance against materialism could be freely let go, the associations dissolved, the opposition pointless. I dislodged the need to criticize what was no longer glaring at me. It's interesting how a hostile atmosphere in a luxurious house can make luxury itself seem to growl.

36

Everyone feels to some degree the fear of being found out – the threat that others might see them for who they really are – and I imagine that, at times, everyone feels themselves to be too inadequate to be loved, too imperfect in comparison to others, too unfit to reveal themselves wholly to others, too low. The cycle persists as much from the silence of love as from loud-spoken antagonism.

If everyone were honest in public, everyone would be in love with everything in life, every fantastical person and every inconsequential fleck of dust. It's common, instead, to be afraid of love. Fear overwhelms the mind with the need to defend itself. Fear prevents love to the extent that the mind, too busy defending itself, can't see the beauty of life, especially as it would be seen had love been admitted and allowed. It's even difficult for people to admit love to a lover. That's hard enough, and so it's much harder to admit to loving a stranger. It's easier to find faults, to search a person for errors and imperfections to criticize. It takes a great deal of strength to stand before the world unafraid and forget the errors and imperfections, to love in spite of fear.

37

One thing I've learned is that the being has no real views, but rather a great depth of empathetic understanding. It's unconditioned, nonjudgmental, and makes no criticisms. Instead of views, moment by moment revelation is its substance, like a perpetual burgeoning in which everything is forever new, a comfortable resting place.

The being has no attachments. Without attachments, a view seems more like a well-practiced habit, a conditioned mental behavior. Egotism and its intellectual possessions slip into the past. No thoughts are very important, they're just fragments of a conditioned subjectivity, and there's no egotism to cling to them as superior. Views that lead to hostilities, the sort with all manner of egotism, are experienced as the attachments of a conflicted self and let go. They might even appear absurd, because the often overzealous importance once placed on them vanishes.

Conflicts fall away because without the self, no views exist that can divide things into good or bad. Therefore, on a higher level, no ideologies can have an antithesis, because ideologies themselves become absurdities, rejected and ignored. Views dissipate like the mist on a mountainside, as quickly as the mind dissipates, until only a wide-awake presence without opposition or partiality rests in the moment, full of empathetic understanding, unconditioned, nonjudgmental, uncritical, full of a joyful presence at all hours. In that state, egotism dies, conflicts cease to be important, and the essence of everything reveals itself in a sudden ecstatic explosion.

38

One night I had a dream. I was bodiless. I was hovering in the midst of a great purple space that enveloped me and engulfed everything. The space was as vast as the night, like a great throbbing texture that went on and on everywhere around me.

Images materialized in the space. They appeared before me and then moved toward me. Then, something strange happened. Suddenly, hundreds of the images flew into my mind. Then a thousand more. They flew from the purple space directly into me, rushing through my senses, into my synapses, with a sudden jolt like lightning entering my consciousness.

It was as if someone had struck me on the temple and in an instant my mind had exploded with awareness, a sudden quickening too impossible for language or even intelligibility.

The images were abstract, like arcane symbols or ancient runes, with size and shape and weight. But they entered my mind with the force of fully formed ideas. It was, in a sense, as if I were reading a strange text in which symbols conveyed great bursts of information directly into my mind.

I could feel the presence of a mind behind what I saw. I was reading a book that was, more or less, alive, a living being. And while it went on, I could feel the ideas themselves. In spite of having no words to describe them, I could feel them with an understanding equal to intellectual understanding. Emotional knowledge. An emotional thought stream.

For what seemed like hours, the images raced into me. They were dreams, illuminations, entire philosophies. Time was indiscernible in the onslaught. A year might have passed. A decade. Then all of time on earth erupted in my brain: a century, a millennium; the whole of existent reality on earth, an explosion of interwoven connectivity, of minute puzzle pieces that could be seen all at once or taken apart for individual examination.

It was time on earth in one solid spasm. It was the beating heart composed of all living creatures, every organism that had existed. It was every distance outward and every distance inward, collapsed, the embodiment of everything, the pulse of a billion lives, a single heart belonging to a single multitude.

Then, I woke up. I struggled to retain what just a moment before I had held so completely in my mind. But it was impossible. It was the eternities of everything, the being that enveloped all beings and was all beings. It was incomprehensible to my waking mind. Instead, it was a feeling emblazoned in my consciousness.

No words can describe such a dream. To see the world as a whole stretching backward in time to the beginning, like the tree I saw that night along the mountain path, with all the experiences of history viewed – laments, misfortunes, tragedies, joys, pleasures, loves – might as well be an education, like shared poetry written by the whole of the human race, with the purpose of the education being emotional knowledge.

39

You forgive everyone. People come with stories that explain why they are the way they are. It's usually the same: a matter of not having received the love they needed, and sometimes the drastic ways they've attempted to relieve themselves of the feeling of being unlovable. To withhold love from people because they've not received enough love – that's what's made them troubled, or worse, in the first place.

Moreover, the being floats in an infinitude of emptiness in which nothing is or can be better than anything else. It drifts through it, drifts off into a starry-eyed trance, blissful and at peace, soaring through the unbound, like a lucid dream. With nothing better than anything else and nothing less than anything else, the being accepts everyone with an elated, inexhaustible, unconditional affection, which in most cases is sorely needed.

40

All I see of other people with my eyes is a body, a face, their physical reality, which hardly expresses what's inside them. There are immense landscapes inside them, full of love and hate, bliss and terror, peace and suffering. Entire personalities have been constructed. All manner of thoughts and memories circulate in their minds.

In ordinary circumstances, it doesn't occur to me that others are feeling what I'm feeling, the immense love I feel for them. It slips from my mind. Because I can't see inside them. But the likelihood is that they're burying it. I don't show it. I usually bury it when in public. They don't show it either, and likewise, it's probably buried.

The external world presents an obstacle for the internal world to transcend. All the anxieties it gives rise to make it easier to limit the expression of affection, to interact with others on a superficial level. It leads people to feel alone and unlike others. Others appear to have little happening on a deeper level. Because what they feel inside is rarely expressed in public.

But nor do I express it in public. To assume I'm any different and that my buried feelings aren't shared by others is an entirely erroneous approach. If I could see inside the hearts of others, I'd see that people aren't how they act. How they act is not all they are. Certainly they wear masks to protect themselves, though they're not frauds either. They're scared, naturally. But I'm no different. If I consider what they feel, it's the same thing I feel, and the same thing I hide.

As a rule, I should anticipate the being in them and expect what it feels. I might find it easy to learn to reflexively act with affection. Because once the being comes into contact with other beings, the undercurrent pulls them together. The illusory falls away. Unreality is sloughed off. Everything is forgotten except the crowd of beings. They're breathtaking, like a panoramic view from atop the mountains. In that fashion, I could spend my life like a dreaming lover who has awakened to discover his beloved is real.

41

When I attempted suicide, I was near death. I lay in a hospital feeling cold, losing consciousness. It went on for hours. My body became icy from time to time. From time to time, my consciousness began to slip off even further. At first, I felt only grief. I felt a deep sadness and complete disgust with the situation. But I needed to find a way to relax, to let go.

As I faced the end, I felt fear, tension, and pain. But even more so I felt emotional pain, a sense of horror at what I'd done. I'd been stumbling about in life. I'd been deranged, suffering acutely, looking for an escape. I'd slipped into an unhealthy routine, which eventually resulted in my having allowed the world to affect me with despair.

In order to relax, I tried to visualize various situations. Like a walk. Falling in love. None of them worked. I simply lay in the hospital with my mind acutely disturbed and my body fighting against failure. Eventually, my thoughts drifted to the being inside me. It had come out the moment I'd poisoned myself. With a stark entry, it had appeared with all the beauty of a deity, and because of its beauty, I lay in the hospital feeling a sense of horror. As I saw the beauty of my being, I felt horror at having tried to kill it.

It was no small being. It was a vast thunderstorm. My life had for some time been desperate and miserable, but when it came out, the being that had experienced all my suffering was a magnificent thing, a beautiful thing. It was a work of strange art sculpted by the dreamlike. No end. No beginning. It affected me like a drug that brought on bliss.

I lay in the hospital aghast at the thought that it might die, especially at the thought that it might die unknown, never shared, never seen. The whole spirit of existence had come into me and I lay in a hospital bed near death, about to have it erased.

However, I began to relax. Something deeper came to the fore. I began to be filled with peace. The being within me was so beautiful it filled me with a beautiful tranquility. I describe it as beautiful over and over because it was the embodiment of beauty. It was an Adonis sculpted by Michelangelo, with all the softness of polished marble. It was a Romeo with all the gentleness of first love. That was the being. It came to the fore just then with an overpowering love, one which removed all my unhappiness.

Whatever troubles had taken over my life, none of them were painful anymore. I was present before the experiencer; the experiencer was present in me. It was likely the same thing experienced just before death, the miraculous suddenly apparent in everything because the being rises to the surface with a loving disposition. I didn't lose consciousness. Rather, I lay in the hospital entranced by the spell the thing had cast.

When it was over, I'd survived. My ears rang and I was weak from the overdose. But I left the hospital well-supplied for a lifetime of hardship. For the being in me was unbreakable. It was a celebration of life. When I concentrate, I see its traces in my life. I delve into the structures of my mind and experience firsthand what lies beneath. It's always there waiting. I'm unsure if it ever dies. It comes on like consciousness in the midst of sleep. I stay with it for a time.

42

On the night when my self fell away, my eyes opened. My mind was unshackled. I sat with the unconditioned, an ever-present essence that seemed to belong to another time-scape. A strange madness entered my brain, and it has remained with me to some degree ever since. Face to face with the unknown, experiencing the unknown directly, I felt the world itself fall to pieces, with a great shattering I could feel in my limbs, and I changed. Livid and wide-eyed, aghast and enthralled, terrified and in bliss, I saw the purification of everything, the healing of my broken self, the transformation of my suffering into bliss, and then back again. I saw pleasure and pain in large amounts, shocking my brain.

I'd attained a state of being. It was perhaps a bit of the transcendent, perhaps a loss of egotism. And yet, what came back were the same old dark creatures. They frightened me back to earth. Strange and disquieting thoughts. They began to race through my mind. Feelings of unworthiness. Feelings of shame. A whole slew of unpleasant things. They cast me downward into doubt.

My inner voice turned against me. My surface self became eerie, conjuring apparitions and disturbing ghosts that flitted about in the corners of my thoughts. Fearful images built up within me, tore at my insides. These things I'd been ignorant of. I'd never seen into the darkest corners. It was impossible to steady my pulse. I had to breathe deeply in order to relax. My feelings were erratic: blissful, joyful, tingling, electric feelings ran through my limbs; infinite love; then terror, alarm, the threatening vastness of the unknown.

I went inside and lay about, hour after hour. I'd crossed over and released the subterranean reaches of my unconscious self. I'd descended far and untangled the dark roots only to find an entire universe of darkness. I had no refuge, and the very idea of peace seemed lost for good. It made a mess of me. My hands trembled, my knees were weak, so weak I staggered when I went for water. As I drank a glass of water in the bathroom, my face looked back at me from the mirror like a punishment. My eyes were dark. Sickly. I was Dorian Gray, painted in livid colors, sick in heart and mind, demented. My mind was full of terror, as if I'd seen my greatest fear trying to enter. My unconsciousness had risen to the surface, my most primitive shadow self was in collision with everything I imagined myself to be.

It was the dark night of the soul, that place at the furthest edge of night. When the self is threatened to be disposed of, it struggles with the strength of madness to return to control. And I lost, completely. A blinding white light burnt into every dark, hidden crevice in my skull. I needed to escape the madness, the derangement and the annihilation of my rationality. Confused and frenzied, I thought of dying. My mind was filled with a nagging thought that refused to be quieted: "Why not kill yourself?" It was like a thousand arrows. It was like a primal scream.

It was not the spectacular enlightenment I'd imagined. There was a darkness to it. Refusing to let go, my dying self exercised supernatural strength, reduced me to a shivering pile, and I went insane. My mind was taken over by more primitive forces. They were instinctive. They were primal. Fear. Bare and faceless and horrific. It swept through me for hours, took complete possession, and the night went on into nightmares.

Such an experience has an irrevocable effect. Half-sick and demented, I saw the inexplicable, the strange metaphysics of the unconditioned and the sinister beauty of a demon at my throat. I was enclosed in the strangeness of the hideous and sublime universe, which was like a darkness that illuminated, a living shadow, a pale specter of impeccable beauty, a ghost made of the absence of light that was the brightest light. My ears rang with its singing, and it hurt like a siren's song.

It's impossible to describe. Horrification came into me as suddenly as bliss. In moments, I was terrified. It was then replaced by awe. Everything was perfect and frightening. Everything was pure and diseased. Everywhere in my vision was the divine and its antithesis. I looked out the window. An October sky, deep and dismal. The wind hissed through the cracks in the windowsill. The walls creaked. A film of sweat covered my face. And it seemed as if I'd died a thousand years ago. Throughout, I was feverish, but an uncanny crispness permeated the room. I felt my body grow hot then cold. Eventually, I had to get out, so I went for a walk.

But the walls of the buildings, the cement of the sidewalk, the black asphalt of the street breathed as if horribly alive. And everything was so dreadfully silent. The night looked like a black temple, an open archway that led to nothingness, emptiness, with stars overhead on fire like terrifying gods.

All the while, my heart beat thunderously, a strange madness boiled within me, and life seemed to have frozen in time, come to a halt, even vanished. I was alone descending step by step into a death of consciousness. A moment later, my interior was filled with extraordinary feelings. Every sensation was intensified. I staggered about in a strangely elated torment, out of my wits, ecstatic, trying to put a name to things, but my only language was the babble of a newborn. It was impossible for anything to be ordinary. The fragrance of flowers was everywhere in the air, and when I smelled it, I could feel a pulse. The flowers and everything else was made up of multitudes of deities, deified every moment, and I was in the midst of the origination of everything. All that was before me was a beautiful behemoth, lit up one moment by life and the next by the horrible immensity of the whole universe.

43

Bliss and terror appear to be coupled in me. After the bliss, the ecstatic sense of presence inside me, my mind began to race and fight and frighten me back into myself. When I was face to face with the underlying source of myself, along with it came horrified sensations, like ghosts walked before me. When the veil of reality was pushed aside, a fevered imagination, a mind-bending sense of unreality, the feeling that everything was distorted and dangerous instantly began to work to bring me back.

One moment, my body was loose, I was sitting in the presence beneath everything, and it was like being in the presence of an infinite soul. The next moment my muscles tightened, I lost my mind to worries, anxiety, shame, while every shadow crept about me with diseased claws, threatening to attack.

From the zenith of my spiritual experience, which was a direct experience of the unconditioned, I plummeted headfirst off the cliffside. An abyss swallowed me up. When my surface self had nearly been stopped dead, I was directed inevitably toward fear, because I'd begun the whole thing still bound by fear. I might suppose I wasn't pure enough. But in truth what's required is not purity, but to be free even from purity.

44

I remember what it was. The experience was almost supernatural. Briefly, my mind ceased to function. Nothing had a name. My voice had no language. All I'd thought I was fell apart, belonged to a historical self. My entire psychological makeup disintegrated, leaving no meanings, no sense of self and therefore no memory of what things had meant before.

The unconditioned was a mirror without an image. It was a presence in front of that mirror, bodiless, boundless, surrounded by a whirling tornado. At the eye of the storm, there was only peace, elation, even giddiness. Then it was over. The storm caught up with me, drew me back into the chaos, and I returned to my deformed consciousness with only a memory of what it was like to sit for a while in nothingness, emptiness, free of all cognizable meaning.

The unconditioned was the sort of eternal silence that might be found at the center of the universe. A bodiless essence with a silent voice without a language, it spoke with silence and meant everything. It had a pair of observing eyes like a vast field, as expansive as a supernova stretching forever, and they gazed down upon me where I sat alone. I faced it while experiencing the erasure expected upon dying, that eternal absence of the self and its return to blackness, to nothingness as it was before, to nonexistence, to death, but suddenly the entire universe poured into my dying mouth, filled up my body, and while my surface self was drowning, my being breathed it in like a baby in the womb. The unconditioned was joy, and a terrifying macrocosmic presence, the eternal disembodied field of awe, watching like living solitude.

45

I went away alone. I sought out the underlying causes of my fears. I found something, and the hidden in my brain came pouring out in a paroxysm of unstable, wide-eyed bliss. Does it often happen so suddenly? The unconditioned was right there in my room as a presence that obliterated. Nothing was there to be grasped. No learning was required. The root of my identity came out. A flower. A mandala. Discoveries upon discoveries mounted and mounted. The lines of my thinking became clearer and clearer. In a few moments, years of thought came spilling out, everything about myself became easy to understand. I was emotionally distorted, happy then sad, blissful then in terror. My mind comforted me and scolded me. I lay in bed for four days, eating only a few potatoes. I'm unsure how sick I was.

What was left of me by the end was nothing. Everything removed. My sense of self gone like a flash of lightning. Bliss and terror. Bliss and terror. I felt the essence that permeated all things. My being became part of nothingness interconnected, which was immensity, the endlessness of the infinitesimal and the conjoining of the previous moment with every sliver of the universal. Nothing was excluded. For four days, with a thrumming in my ears, I crossed paths with it, my limbs languid and my blood intoxicated. Stumbling through the dark, I searched for a way to understand what couldn't be understood. The sum of the parts made something vast. It spanned from the beginning to the end and swam with possible interpretations.

46

Behind each moment, there's a substance, and it threads through life. Behind every veil, there's something that breathes through the veil. Behind the curtain, a world with more reality than anything previously imagined. There's the surface above and the depths below.

When I sit alone in a dimly lit room, when I go into the night and stare up into the billions of stars, when I'm alone with my face pressed against the glass looking into the impenetrable night, what I feel is closer to what I am than anything that's ever happened on the surface. My senses awaken and my mind is enlightened. My being is clear in the dark, until I return to the ordinary world, at which time it goes back to the unknown absence from which it came.

The being lies within, well-supplied for a lavish century of celebration, a thorough binging on life. It watched me wake this morning, watched me make my coffee and smoke my cigarettes, watched as I showered and brushed my teeth, looked at me in the mirror, unraveling moment by moment until I failed to remember to be with it. Then it was gone, and I was lulled to the kind of waking sleep that makes the day pass.

It would be nice to free myself of all illusions. However, the most extravagant surgery couldn't dislodge the proper spot in my brain that makes the ordinary world seem real, even necessary, because as of yet nobody knows just where that's located. But underneath, an essence awaits my arrival. I detect the faintest sensation of it and a moment later I brace myself because all of life is about to become sublime.

47

The being is fearless. Its love is fearless. To bring the being's fearless love into my daily life while I'm still alive is a delightful objective. While all the world seems illusory, that fearless love seems to be a powerful representation of the otherworldly, the being beneath the mundane surface. I tend to have more faith in the underground bloodstream than I do in all the surface troubles of life. The cacophony of a city street is hardly making a clamor for love, but love is clearly more beautiful than anything else, and more necessary. The street rather clangs with the kind of necessity that wears people down to nothing. By the end of the day, they have no energy left, no strength to defend against stress, and trouble defeats them far more easily. Love remains needed, like an antidote for the unhappy and worn.

Most important is for me to take steps toward a peaceful, contented, affectionate state of mind. A fearless state of mind. In such a state of mind, I could soothe myself and uplift my spirits until it would be commonplace for me to stand fearlessly in a crowd in love with complete strangers. My habits are those of a renunciate; I don't care much for participating in human systems, but I've reconciled myself as much as I'm able with life. I don't expect to find more peace of mind than I already have. But it's fitting that I should love without fear. I should bring that profound and fearless love up from the depths and distribute it freely, if possible.

Much more fearlessness has come into my life. Often, people are nearly aglow with the divine when I look at them. I've shifted my attention from the surface to what lies within. I believe they're beautiful, and so they are incredibly beautiful. My perception of life penetrates down into the majestic that lies within, and so like an inquisitive child fascinated with living creatures, I look upon people with a complete sense of their miraculousness. They're resplendent. The life inside them glows. Like summer flowers lying in the sun, they illuminate the cities with a bright array of magical faces.

I retain self-control. I'm too reserved to offer hugs to strangers, though I admire those who do. I'm too frightened still. I imagine everyone is to some degree. But sometimes I observe people until the magnificence of life is clearly embodied by them, till all the universe seems to have coalesced into their presence at the precise moment I'm looking. I see them all as dignified royalty, each possessing a soft grace in the depths of their beings, and I'm lost to a sudden mysticism, the same as I am in the woods among the trees, in the fields among the flowers, with the vibrance of life surrounding me, only it's the noble grandeur of human beings that comes up from the earth.

My days are often tranquil, full of those lulled moments when euphoria revives. Love often enlivens my mind, alights every-thing in my thoughts, and it's worth abandoning myself to it for several long hours. I have nowhere to take it, nobody to give it to. But the beginning of my quest has concluded and the fondness I have for the human race is inexhaustible. It's a healthy sanctuary everywhere around me when I walk the earth as if it were a temple full of gods.

I suppose they're right who say the self must be annihilated and then rebuilt, and the same for those who say love is the cure. I've traveled as a ghost, alone, and have discovered the being within all things. Sometimes I stand in a crowd with an abstract smile at the center of my being directed at everyone nearby, watching from a placid inwardness. I stand still while the world whirls around me like a tornado. It's sometimes panicked and grasping for peace, and though I'd like to soothe the suffering when I see it, I can only return to my room and contemplate.

I've found my solution to the problem of being, my own individual answer, a satisfactory interpretation of the Rorschach inkblot. Sometimes I burst into a silence that has nothing but love in it, alone in my room, and for a time I follow my own private religion. In my imagination, I devote myself to every person with utmost adoration, even if I'm all alone behind closed doors in the quiet.

48

My life continues onward from here. Where it might lead, I don't know. All my life I've searched through my mind and have discovered inside it the dark and the radiant. Less conflict plagues me these days than it did when I was young, and I'm much more comfortable and at peace than I was for decades before.

I dream miraculous dreams. Strange worlds like mandalas made of light appear for me to explore. I have conversations with dreamy deities I know are just dreams but who show me incredible things that increase my store of ease. I read strange books full of mysterious teachings while I sleep, for hours on end, my eyes moving back and forth beneath my eyelids. I awaken in a good mood, and a glow of pleasant feelings lasts all morning. No nightmares ever come, just a brilliance and a light that creates shapes, forms images, and in which I consider the implications of another, different, otherworldly life, which is nonetheless inextricably linked to this one. I've been a talented dreamer.

Every person can find that otherworldly life. It's a freely loving thing. Without conditions, it's the source of free love. No judgments. No prejudices. No biases. No better than or less than. No worthy or unworthy. That being behind the gauzy veil of existence has treated me with great benevolence. I've met a companion, a friend in it, one who has a lot of love, and I lie about in dreams that induce a soporific but thoughtful trance, communicating with it, in a way.

While I've experienced firsthand the horror of what lies in my darker self, it seems the experience I had of the unconditioned freed me to a great extent. Afterward, it elevated my health and my well-being. As in the lucid dream that comes on with ego-death, everything makes sense in its own way, even if the only sense needed is the rapture discovered in being.

Rapture waits in there. Being is an ever-present, lucid moment underlying all things, and it feels the depth and breadth of unconditional love. I've changed by degrees, with little adjustments throughout my day, and I change still, day by day, because of my having experienced the falling away of things other than the being.

In the end, I breathe easier in public. I look at others and see deeper than their faces alone. I find the inherent in them. When strangers pass me in the street, under the surface of the illusion, the observer is always present in them, like gods carved out of jade, statuesque figures that inspire the utmost reverence. The divine shines from everyone in the street. I can think of nothing better than to occupy my thoughts with it.

I've been so frightened. I'm out of my element in the ordinary world. I cultivate my dreams because I can rest peacefully in them. They've enriched my experience of the world, turning me on to gentler modes of living that make it easier for me to face a crowd. It's essential that I dig down into the inward being, because my preference is tranquility. I simply ignore the surface of life. But my interior reverie is striving to rise to the surface and become my outward character.

As a result, for instance, I care very little these days about things others might take offense to. I don't pay attention anymore to the hostility I might encounter on the street. I'm gentle toward strangers, more and more. My surface is becoming more like the being inside me. I accept others unconditionally. I do my best to make no judgments, and I do my best to steer away from the banality of criticism. I try to use my knowledge of the unconditioned being within as a model for my exterior life. I try to dress up in its leisurely clothes, speak with its self-assured tenderness, act with its patient and warm composure. I've been changing gradually, moving toward fearlessness, warm expressiveness, painstaking freedom, and the immaterial inwardness I practice is what's causing the changes. A dichotomy still exists in me. There's a split between my surface self and the being within. But I'm drawn inward more and more, and my interior is moving upward toward a unification, an external expression of my being.

49

I think there's a great deal more to existence than what's human and perceivable. Things creep up on me late at night. I feel the sensation of a vast undercurrent to life, and it enlivens me. A lavish night under the stars with a bottle of wine does the same. I stagger about in the dark in touch with my interior.

Feverish and drinking to excess, I feel the darkness like vast space, and I'm alone in it, energized by the gray and the black, with the magical over my head, a multitude of mysteries. There's no discernible meaning to it, no comprehensible sense, no overarching theme that I'm aware of. But it brings me closer to what's within, the spark of awe for all things existing. It makes me feel alive, softer in my limbs and in my eyes, and a gentleness washes over me. A feeling of benevolence intimates itself just beneath the veil, coming closer and closer.

The being lives in a comfortable leisure, wanting nothing, needing nothing. As the world goes on, the being rests, sitting idly without competition or conflict, wanting only to luxuriate in a free life, without attachments, without possessions, without intellectual possessions above all. No clinging to ideas. No right vs. wrong. No righteousness vs. unrighteousness. No need to prove itself to the competition. No need to tell others what they should do with their lives. When experienced, all else falls away, all the difficulties of existence and all the ways in which people compete, leaving only boundless love, a state of bliss that has no conflict in it.

It was my initiation into love. It drew me downward, away from physical realities, inward. Far underneath, a pulse beat, the central core of every living thing. From my first aimless wanderings I was drawn to it, and whatever method I exercised to seek freedom from my troubles, I found myself delving down toward it. The witness in me may have been the director all along, prodding me along. My impulses brought me out into the dark, but it's possible some intuition was being raised into my awareness from the depths of myself, in anticipation of my arrival.

When the rain came hard, I instantly went out to discover what it felt like. When the wind swept over the mountains, I had to stand in it and watch the trees lashing. I was preparing myself. Until eventually I found the resplendent. Now, I find my interior rising up, making itself known. I see the same in others, and then I'm in full bloom.

These days, I look more and more longingly at people, less afraid of them. The quest might have had winding roads, as a traveler I might not have known where to go at all, but something deeper has likely been breathing a wind at my back all along. And now, I see a collective humanity made of the same elemental essence. Wherever I go, I carry it in myself too. So that wherever I go, I can sink down, look out from my interior, fearless of the interior in others. Love cancels fear. I expect my first impulse toward freedom was actually the impetus to seek out a manner of loving. Perhaps it's an idiosyncratic one. Carefully, I looked into myself, and the expression that came about was a meditation on the majestic, the majestic inside all things, the untroubled, fearless, sanctified refuge of the being.

50

My self-awareness is limited. I go about my day only partially aware of the physical world around me. Often I pay too little attention to external situations. I'm lost in the metaphysical insides of myself, submerged in the subterranean world beneath the unreality of the surface. I become lost in my fantasies and depart from existence like an amnesiac who doesn't recognize reality as reality. I find my real world underneath.

But I no longer feel exiled. I feel in possession of the facts. Life is a painful experience some of the time, but beneath the ordinary are the depths that have brought me into an awareness of an all-encompassing love. It's a love that shows every sign of peace, provides delight, hints at oneness, and creates the impression that life and the world are in every aspect divine.

Every face is carved from holy stone. Every gesture of every person is part of an energetic universe that displays itself moment by moment like an awe-inspiring work of the most dazzling art. It makes me brave enough to admit love. And uplifted enough to see the lovableness of others. I'm optimistic enough to see that something miraculous is happening on earth, and I feel compelled to express it, in some way, like I'm a visitor to a museum standing before a painting of the world and I long to celebrate it with my companions. A few breaths might come out: Ah! That's it! That's the world! That's life!

The fields, the sunlight, the stars, the moon, the creatures everywhere, the people everywhere: I feel no enmity at this stage of my life, because the world fills me with joy. Rather, I feel affectionately toward things, toward people as a whole and people as individuals. I feel an ecstatic pleasure because of the invisible, the awesome stature of the sublime within, and it guides me along, dwells in my dreams, causes me to devote a great deal of my time to simply imagining, like a painter planning a terrific canvas that might express the whole of the human spirit. Life thrives with a vigorous pulse. The hillsides are vibrant, the nights are vibrant, and what moves inside the human spirit is vibrant.

I hide all these feelings. More often than not. Just like everyone. But because I hide them, I know others at times feel the same zeal for life, hidden too. Overcoming the obstacle of the exterior is nearly impossible. It presents a wall that, with great strength, resists being breached. I remind myself therefore that if all this is within me, it's within everybody, here and there, hidden away, discovered in soulful moments when the spell entrances and calms the nerves, when the fears subside and walking down a street in broad daylight is like a lucid dream.

I walk about silently in public but I feel all this inside. I'm on the verge of love, but I keep it secret. I want to say: I love you very much. You are here with me. I may have been too downcast to show you what I wanted to show you. But at the end of it all, I see in my being what I feel in your being. I'd say it if I had no fear, if I could. I'd say it to everyone in the street. I think without all the fear, everyone would say it with plain voices, until naturally everyone would be conscious of others just as they're conscious of themselves, with the same intimacy.

A blooming street of faces even in the drizzling rain is what I'd love to see, even if I do nothing to bring it about myself. I fall into my trances and fantasies, I feel less fear than ever, but my impairment is the same as anyone's. I'm split. My exterior is a different person, full of fright and hesitation, with unconscious habits like those of a banal, ceaselessly working machine. He watches the blooming roses but merely watches them, while my being is the one who feels them. I sense the immensity of all that goes on before my eyes, but my external individuality expresses little of my interior, it simply carries on as before.

Though there's time enough to teach him the internal. My interior might mentor my exterior. Here at the end, I approach toward fearlessness. I feel love for everyone and everything without exception. Nothing would be more satisfying than for my interior to rise up and be the mannerisms of my exterior.

51

I expect the pursuit of freedom lasts a lifetime. Every layer I peel off the surface reveals another layer, a deeper intricacy, a more puzzling puzzle. Every step is like the first step on a road traveled ten thousand times. I learn, I grow, but it's a continual beginning. I begin again and again, again and again. Nevertheless, I've changed. People were once only images to me, surfaces, separate universes indifferent to my own, and they were frightening. They might as well have been clockworks, because I'd hardly imagined the essence permeating them. While here after all my experiences, the being is quite visible in every individual. I see it like the glow of health in a face. It feels as if every cell in every person were luminous to my inner eye. They radiate like magic, and I want to move nearer to people rather than to retreat. I look into the faces of strangers and my senses heighten: whoever lies beneath those faces is holy.

I look at people because they're beautiful, and I see something, a sudden glance from behind the veil. It's a ghost, the same as me, a metaphysical awareness beneath the surface. It's over there, where a man is sweeping dirt outside an office. It's in the woman passing beside me on her way down the street. I see it in the leaves shimmering in the sun. I see it everywhere in everything. Something strange. The beloved. Drifting from being to being. Across the street, there's a woman eating her lunch on a park bench. She's small, hunched over, lost in her own dream – and I love her. What I see is crystal clear: a merging, everything composed of everything, life composed of life, the mystical perceivable when in love.

Nevertheless, while my being lies inside restfully, in an unconditioned space, there's a split: I'm one person on the surface, sometimes trembling. My mind is a twosome. The watcher waits within. My being is continually contented and pleased with everything. He's an abstract dreamer, lying about at all hours in silence and leisure, who likely brought me deliberately to the remote places of the world to show me where he could be found. In solitude, I'm him. In my interior, I'm his tranquility. I can remember entire nights when he rose up and transformed me. He drew my attention to the vastness in everything, inherent in the cells of flowers as much as in the starry sky. He's not as passive as might be imagined, but instead reminds me with a languid rapture to engage myself with the underlying nature that exists within. There's a veil. Beneath it is a tender, unconditioned being that gazes out lovingly. It belongs to everything.